"Izabela Grabowska and Agata Jastrzebowski insightful discussion of the state of knowledge ... research topics: the acquisition, transfer and utilisation of human capital by international migrants and returned migrants. They weave theoretical discussion with a review of empirical research in two of the 'hot spots' of labour migration, Central Europe and Mexico, ranging from overviews to micro case studies that draw on their own extensive research. The volume is both an invaluable starting point for researchers new to the field, and a stimulus for more advanced researchers to rethink their understanding of this field."

Professor Allan Williams, University of Surrey, SHTM, Faculty of Business, Economics and Law

"This is indispensable reading on the acquisition and transfer of human capital across international boundaries, and the implications for local development. The authors provide a thought-provoking theoretical discussion on the topic, and then explore the ways in which researchers have applied it in different national contexts. The authors' impressive survey of the empirical literature on the topic demonstrates the ways in which different migrant groups – from women to men to professionals to those with little schooling – mobilize human capital to enhance economic opportunities. *Migration and the Transfer of Human Capital* is an essential read for students, scholars, and policymakers alike."

Professor Jacqueline Maria Hagan, Kenan Distinguished Professor of Sociology Fellow, Carolina Population Center, The University of North Carolina, Chapel Hill

Migration and the Transfer of Informal Human Capital

This book explores the intangible human capital which international migrants bring with them and develop further when working and living abroad, drawing on case studies and original data from Central Europe and Mexico–USA.

The book demonstrates that despite the fact that many international migrants might be working in their destination countries at a level below their formal qualifications, or else might be formally unskilled, but with practical non-validated skills, they can still acquire and enhance considerable informal human capital in the form of mind skills, soft skills, maker skills and life skills. The book analyses how migration-impacted informal human capital (MigCap) is acquired and enhanced as a result of international migration and what the opportunity and constraint structures are for their acquisitions and transfers. Adopting a comprehensive perspective, the book investigates how migration-impacted informal human capital is transferred by migrants between localities and areas of human actions and activities.

Moving beyond the focus on migration as a source of economic capital, this book demonstrates that learning by observing, communicating and doing with others, embedded in social relations can facilitate the enhancement of intangible human capital among both skilled and unskilled migrants. It will be of interest to researchers of migration, sociology, economics, management and business studies, and other related social science disciplines.

Izabela Grabowska is a sociologist and economist, full professor of social sciences and former IMISCOE board member. She specialises in international migration, human capital and social remittances. She is a professor at Kozminski University, Central Europe.

Agata Jastrzebowska is a social psychologist, assistant professor, expert in applied doctorates and leader of the educational all-encompassing campaign "Speak to me kindly". She specialises in Person-Job fit. She is a post-doc at Kozminski University, Central Europe.

Routledge Studies in Development, Mobilities and Migration

This series is dedicated to the growing and important area of mobilities and migration, particularly through the lens of international development. It promotes innovative and interdisciplinary research targeted at a global readership. The series welcomes submissions from established and junior authors on cutting-edge and high-level research on key topics that feature in global news and public debate.

These include the so called European migration crisis; famine in the Horn of Africa; riots; environmental migration; development-induced displacement and resettlement; livelihood transformations; people-trafficking; health and infectious diseases; employment; South-South migration; population growth; children's wellbeing; marriage and family; food security; the global financial crisis; drugs wars; and other contemporary crisis.

Family Practices in Migration
Everyday Lives and Relationships
Edited by Martha Montero-Sieburth, Rosa Mas Giralt, Noemi Garcia-Arjona and Joaquín Eguren

Student Migration from Eastern to Western Europe
Mette Ginnerskov-Dahlberg

Migration and the Transfer of Informal Human Capital
Insights from Central Europe and Mexico
Izabela Grabowska and Agata Jastrzebowska

For more information about this series, please visit: www.routledge.com/ Routledge-Studies-in-Development-Mobilities-and-Migration/book-series/ RSDM

Migration and the Transfer of Informal Human Capital

Insights from Central Europe and Mexico

Izabela Grabowska and
Agata Jastrzebowska

Routledge
Taylor & Francis Group

LONDON AND NEW YORK

Funded by National Science Centre Poland Grant No. 2017/27/L/
HS6/03261

First published 2022
by Routledge
4 Park Square, Milton Park, Abingdon, Oxon OX14 4RN

and by Routledge
605 Third Avenue, New York, NY 10158

*Routledge is an imprint of the Taylor & Francis Group, an informal
business*

British Library Cataloguing in Publication Data
A catalogue record for this book is available from the British Library

Library of Congress Cataloging-in-Publication Data
Names: Grabowska, Izabela, author. | Jastrzebowska, Agata, author.
Title: Migration and the transfer of informal human capital : insights
from Central Europe and Mexico / Izabela Grabowska and Agata
Jastrzebowska.
Description: Abingdon, Oxon ; New York, NY : Routledge, 2022. |
Series: Routledge studies in development, mobilities and migration |
Includes bibliographical references and index.
Subjects: LCSH: Human capital--Mexico. | Human capital--Europe,
Central. | Emigration and immigration.
Classification: LCC HD4904.7 .G655 2022 (print) | LCC HD4904.7
(ebook) | DDC 658.300943--dc23
LC record available at https://lccn.loc.gov/2021034724
LC ebook record available at https://lccn.loc.gov/2021034725

ISBN: 978-0-367-82031-2 (hbk)
ISBN: 978-1-032-18224-7 (pbk)
ISBN: 978-1-003-01154-5 (ebk)

DOI: 10.4324/9781003011545

Typeset in Times New Roman
by Taylor & Francis Books

Contents

1 Introduction

As Tokarczuk in *Books of Jacob* wrote:

> It is good not to understand the language, not to understand customs,
> to glide like a ghost among others who are distant and unrecogniz-
> able. Then a special wisdom gets awaken – an ability of guessing and
> grasping unobvious. It is then that sharpness and perceptiveness are
> also awakened. A human who is a stranger gains a new point of view,
> becomes, whether a person likes it or not, a peculiar sage (...) Only a
> strangers truly understands what the world is.[1]

Our whole lives we have been raised with the notion that "international
journeys educate" and that by grasping these opportunities we are able
to open up our minds to the world. The entire idea behind the 19th-
century Grand Tour was to travel to the principal cities and places of
interest in Europe, considered to be an essential part of the education
of young adults of good breeding and fortune. It is different however
for Central Europeans and Mexicans, who are the main focus of this
book. These groups primarily travel to other countries for work, usually
for hard work.

Can we say that international migration is a school of life? What dis-
tinguishes migration from other "school of life" experiences? Spending
time in other cultural contexts allows us to learn things about ourselves,
others, relationships, work, that we were never taught at school. Migrants
can be seen as onlookers who can, through their experience gained abroad,
bring a perspective which was muted in familiar context. There is a difference between watching the world through a keyhole and seeing it
through an open door.

> I would probably advise everyone [to go abroad for some time],
> because I, for example, was terribly shy, and going abroad, however, I

DOI: 10.4324/9781003011545-1

had to overcome a certain shyness or even such fear of people, because I had to go and deal with myself. So things like: go, go through all these gates, which was not so easy, go to do something, and a different culture in general (…) this is an amazing school of life.

A female migrant from Poland, middle town, born 1982

Many of the interviewees in this book, especially those in their twenties and thirties, said that migration equipped them with the tools to survive and thrive in the world. For some, migration had served as a crash course in life.

After long period of studying that international migration influences human capital in the situations that migrants usually underperform in the receiving labour markets because they often work below their formal qualifications and earn much less than natives, and are therefore "wasting their brains", we would now like to take an in-depth look at the other side of the coin of human capital and migration. Research on migrant human capital and labour market adjustments focus mostly on the "formal institutional settings that produce measurable proxies of human capital, including schooling, professional training, and host country language" (cf. Hagan et al., 2015: 7). These measures do not allow us to say much about migratory informal human capital. As to why this view is mostly so one-sided, this is because the questions asked in these studies mostly concern the formal parts of human capital.

The informal components of human capital are commonly unrecognised and unappreciated, but play a very important role in the labour process and mobility of workers (cf. Hagan et al., 2015: 7). In addition to framing migratory influences on informal human capital, we will try to reconstruct, along with interviewees, the content of these influences and the stages of the process.

We begin this book with a question: how does international migration influence informal human capital, and how can one acquire and transfer it between a destination and an origin? When we use the term "informal human capital" in this book, we mean commonly known soft skills and all non-certified and non-validated skills acquired, developed and enhanced as a result of working and living abroad.

In 2019 and 2021 Izabela conducted three editions of a research-impact course on *Return mobility* in situ and two editions online, as well as one webinar, *Return mobility and pandemic*, for European Public Employment Services, which was funded by the European Commission. Participants were asking how to measure migrants' soft skills and how to "sell" these skills to their potential employers, usually after returning. Agata for many years has been teaching students university courses on soft skills and conducted an extended analysis on person-job competence fit.

In this book we will present a larger statistical picture of migration influences on informal human capital and their geographies, and we will present at a novelistic level of migrants' narratives a broad set of stimuli and effects where some components of informal human capital were formed and developed as a result of international migration. We will take the reader through social processes by which migrants acquire and transfer various resources of informal human capital across migratory courses.

This book is about informal human capital gained by working and living abroad. It demonstrates that despite the fact that the work that international migrants perform in the destination countries is often below their formal, and usually high, level of education (which is common among migrants from the New EU countries (cf. Voitchovsky, 2014; Kaczmarczyk and Tyrowicz, 2015) or below their actual ability given that they are formally not very well-educated but have many practical, non-validated skills (as is often the case with Mexican migrants (cf. Hagan et al. 2015), migrants are nevertheless able to acquire and enhance informal human capital (Williams and Baláž, 2005; Hagan et al., 2015; Grabowska and Jastrzebowska, 2019). This means that there is always room to improve human capital. In other words, migration is not only about gaining economic capital. It is a social process through which migrants acquire, enhance and transfer informal human capital across not only locations but also across stages of life – lifelong learning – and various domains of life – lifewide learning.

In this book, formal human capital covers all certified and formalised aspects of educational attainment, years of schooling, certified qualifications, work experience. The concept also comprises considerations about life and health. Informal human capital therefore covers non-certified human resources, which concern being and acting in the social world and are captured at four interplaying components: mind skills, soft skills, maker skills and life skills.

The key objectives of this book are fivefold: (1) to conceptually frame informal human capital impacted by international migration; (2) to explore the human capital profiles of international migrants, with special focus on the case countries; (3) to identify the relationships between experience with working and living abroad and the informal components of human capital; (4) to analyse how people are exposed to the development of informal human capital, how various components of informal human capital are acquired and enhanced as a result of international migration, and what are the opportunity and constraint structures for the acquisition and transfer of informal human capital; and (5) to explain how migration-affected informal human capital is transferred by migrants between localities and used after all. The background perspective of lifelong and lifewide learning (Jarvis, 2007) help to understand that the outcomes relating to the development of informal human capital through migratory experience might be not immediate, but can instead be postponed and visible in various life domains: work, family, hobbies, public spaces such as parks, libraries, squares and institutions such as offices. It means that socially situated informal learning takes place throughout the whole life and across the various social roles that people perform in life.

Why have we decided to juxtapose the migratory experiences of Central Europeans (mostly Poles, Slovaks and Lithuanians) with those of Mexicans? There are a few reasons behind this choice. Firstly, we want to bring together groups and their human capital-affecting migratory experiences from two sides of the Atlantic Ocean, as this would make the leading argument more universal. Secondly, migration has been shown to affect human capital among both Central European and Mexican migrants, even though the average profiles of both groups, according to OECD (2008), are different – 20 percent of Central European migrants have a university degree and 30 percent primary education, while 70 percent of Mexican migrants have primary education and less than 6 percent tertiary education. Thirdly, because the groups are different, it supports the rationale of the argument regarding the impact of migration on informal human capital.

This book consists of seven chapters, including this introductory invitation to consider the influences of migration on informal human capital.

Chapter 2 is primarily conceptual and is designed to make an inclusive frame for informal human capital influenced by international migration. Starting with discussions on classical concepts of human capital, it also touches on, among other concepts, the human capabilities approach, as well as psychological capital and conservation of resources leading to the proposal of an original concept: *Migration-Impacted Informal Human Capital*.

Chapter 3 focuses on methodology and reflects on challenges in obtaining migration data, collating and explaining sources of data. The analysis model used in this book is also presented, reflecting both acquisition, transfer and obstructing informal human capital. Furthermore, this chapter presents the multi-picture approach presented in this chapter, which consists of (1) *big picture* capturing statistical data; (2) *meso picture* with numerous cross-cases analyses and (3) *micro picture* with stories of migrants.

Chapter 4 uses the multi-picture approach described above to profile Central European and Mexican migrants who fall within the scope of this monograph. This chapter primarily identifies formal human capital characteristics, such as education, labour market performance age and sex.

Chapter 5 is about how, why and which resources of informal human capital are acquired as a result of international migration experience. Chapter 6 discusses the transferral of resources relating to informal human capital between a destination back to an origin country and between various domains of life.

Chapter 7 presents synthesis of informal human capital affected by international migration and conclusions. The chapter also offers data-driven recommendations for both business organisations and public institutions.

This book is the concluding effort of a ten-year research and educational programme on the non-material outcomes of international migration.

Note

1 Nachman in *Book of Comet*. Own translation.

References

Grabowska, I., Jastrzębowska, A. (2019). The impact of migration on human capacities of two generations of Poles: The interplay of the *individual* and the *social* in human capital approaches. *Journal of Ethnic and Migration Studies, Special Issue, 47*(8), 1829–1847. doi:10.1080/1369183X.2019.1679414.

Hagan, J. C., Hernández-León, R., Domonsant, J. C. (2015). *Skills of the "Unskilled". Work and Mobility among Mexican Migrants*. Oakland: University of California Press.

Jarvis, P. (2007). *Globalization, Lifelong Learning and the Learning Society: Sociological Perspectives*. London, New York: Routledge.

Kaczmarczyk, P., Tyrowicz, J. (2015). Winners and losers among skilled migrants: The case of post-accession Polish migrants to the UK. *IZA Discussion Papers, No. 9057.*

OECD Organisation for Economic Co-operation and Development. (2008). *A profile of immigrant populations in the 21st century: data from OECD countries*. Paris: OECD Publishing.

Tokarczuk, O. (2020). *Księgi Jakubowe* [Books of Jacob]. Kraków: Wydawnictwo Literackie.

Voitchovsky, S. (2014). Occupational downgrading and wages of new member states immigrants to Ireland. *International Migration Review, 48*(2), 500–537.

Williams, A. M., Baláž V. (2005). What human capital, which migrants? Returned skilled migration to Slovakia from the UK. *International Migration Review, 39*(2), 439–468.

2 Migration-impacted informal human capital (MigCap)

> A person should migrate to immerse themselves in another liquid. It reformats the mind and gives a wider perspective between the insider and outsider.
> Some immerse themselves more intellectually, others simply practically
>
> (from an anonymous interview)

Introduction

When discussing the impact of international migration on various components of human capital, it is worth briefly outlining its conceptual framework and the research framework needed to present the arguments of this book. Therefore, the chapter is designed to understand how migrants can acquire, enhance, transfer, valorise, mobilise, recognise, maximise and apply their informal human capital through a migratory circuit.

In this book, we study temporary migration, with migration episodes varying from months up to several years, and involving both single and multiple moves. A temporary migration is therefore not linear and also incorporates migrants' return.

This chapter seeks to establish an all-encompassing conceptual framework specifically tailored to *Migration-Impacted Informal Human Capital* (MigCap). The creation of this framework is based on an overview and discussion of the classical human capital approach (Mincer, 1974; Schultz, 1961; Becker, 1962); human capabilities (Sen, 2000, 1997; Nussbaum, 2011) and the aspiration-capabilities framework (Carling and Schewel, 2018; de Haas, 2005); human capacities (Archer, 2018; Smith, 2011); psychological capital, or PsyCap (Luthans and Youssef, 2004) and conservation of resources (Hobfoll, 1989); total human capital (Li et al., 1996; Findlay et al., 1996; Hagan et al., 2014, 2015); and capacities for

DOI: 10.4324/9781003011545-2

reflexivity and life concerns (Archer, 2007). In the following pages of this book, these will be placed in the context of the migratory circuits of representatives of two different origins, located on opposite sides of the world: Central Europeans and Mexicans. Against this backdrop, this book seeks to go beyond the discussion on human capital in relation to Bourdieu's (1986) seminal economic, social, cultural and symbolic capitals as well as Coleman's and Putnam's social capital. We wish to offer a parallel framework – a new interplay of above-mentioned conceptual approaches conceiving the MigCap.

Human capital and migration

Human capital is an ambiguous and multidimensional concept. It refers to the knowledge, information, ideas, competences and health of individuals (Becker, 1994). The concept was created in the 1950s and 1960s (Mincer, 1958; Schultz, 1961; Becker, 1962) and offered a new perspective on people in society and the economy. Becker (1994) wrote that we live in "the era of human capital", which has become, since the 1970s, the most important form of capital in modern economies, and is the key to understanding the international division of labour. Becker also pointed out that although formal education is crucial for human capital, investing in human capital should take place throughout the lives of individuals, which facilitates technological development and learning, also at a distance. Becker (1962) pointed out that what differentiates people's economic and life well-being is related to investments in human capital. Human capital refers to an individual's stock of knowledge, skills and abilities that can be increased by experience and/or investment in education and training.

> By "human capital" we mean the knowledge and skills people possess that enable them to create value in the global economic system. Human capital is not defined solely through formal education and skilling. It can be enhanced over time, growing through use – and depreciating through lack of use – across people's lifetimes.
>
> (Becker, 1993)

> By "human capital" we mean not individuals themselves but the knowledge and skills they possess that enable them to create value in the global economic system. This requires investment both on the side of individuals and by public and private stakeholders across people's lifetimes.
>
> (World Economic Forum, 2017: 1–3)

By improving their skills, health, knowledge, and resilience – their human capital –people can be more productive, flexible, and innovative.

(Central Bank Human Capital Project)[1]

When people talk about or study human capital, most of the time they say or treat human capital as having to do with employees, their knowledge, qualifications, attitudes, abilities, motivation, health, experience and skills. These components have, under given conditions, a specific value on the labour market. It is quite obvious to assess and measure knowledge and qualifications through formal education, confirmed in the form of diplomas and certificates. It is difficult to evaluate the qualitative, soft components of human capital, relating to abilities, including soft skills. There are no diplomas and certificates for these. Instead, soft skills must be socially read, recognised and decoded. Written and oral recommendations are one form of social recognition of soft skills. These days, certified training to stimulate the development of soft skills is being implemented with increasing frequency; however, it seems that natural social situations are the best arena for their acquisition and improvement. One such natural situation is migration.

The impact of international migration on human capital has been a subject of discussion ever since the concept of human capital was formulated in the 1960s, mainly in the field of economics. Scientific discussion began with the creation of economic models focusing on investment in human capital through migration with a deferred rate of return due to the costs that a person must pay when they decide to leave (e.g. Sjaastad, 1962; Harris and Todaro, 1970), and through analyses of the impacts of migration and migrants on wages and positions in the labour market (e.g. Borjas, 2000), in relation to language competences and earnings by migrants (Chiswick and Miller, 2003, 2012; Dustmann, 1999), and in relation to the positive and negative assimilation of migrants in the host country's labour market relating to the transfer of qualifications and language distance (Chiswick and Miller, 2012).

> Human capital is embedded in migrants, but this is given value by how it is articulated through social and economic relationships. Migrants bring human capital into new spaces, may acquire further human capital during migration, and transfer these to other spaces, or back to their spaces of origin in the course of circuits of mobility.
>
> (William, Baláž and Wallace, 2004: 30–31)

The development of migration-specific human capital has been demonstrated to be an effect of circular migration as well as a key facilitator of migratory movements among Mexican migrants to the US (Massey and Espinosa, 1997). The migration-impacted human capital is one of the key tenets in the conceptualisation of the nexus of international migration and human capital (cf. McGarry et al., 2019).

Previous international socio-economic research has established that experience with temporary work abroad can be a form of investment, and thus a source of human capital as well as economic capital (e.g. Arif and Irfan, 1997; Ilahi, 1999; McCormick and Wahba, 2003; Dustmann and Kirschkamp, 2002; Ma, 2002; Carletto and Kilic, 2009; Tomescu-Dubrow, 2015). However, these effects of migration may vary based on the socio-demographic characteristics of the people involved in a migration process, such as gender (Barrett and O'Connell, 2001), opportunities and education abroad (Li and Bray, 2006; Gerhard and Hans, 2017), language (Dustmann, 1999; Chiswick and Miller, 2003) and destination country (Carletto and Kilic, 2009). The research also demonstrates a significant phenomenon in migration processes, namely the selectivity of people who engage in migration (e.g. Chiswick, 1999; Grabowska-Lusińska and Okólski, 2009; Anacka and Fihel, 2012), and thereby also the selectivity of migration effects related to human capital.

We agree with Lulle et al. (2019: 2) that in migration research we should "(...) enrich our understanding of human capital dynamics as constituting more than an economic domain". Various resources evolve through migration, and these may form a distinct "migration capital" (Brickell and Datta, 2011) where other capitals and resources are amplified or constrained due to the nature of migration experiences (Lulle et al., 2019). Migration is more than a means to obtain economic gains for production and consumption purposes. It is a social process through which migrants acquire and develop difficult-to-measure skills and transfer these across their migratory circuit (cf. Hagan et al., 2015). Migratory experiences bring a plethora of opportunities for human capital development. Mobility is a strategy to augment levels of human capital (Khattab and Fox, 2016).

"Research into human capital acquired via migration traditionally has tended to concentrate on the acquisition of (measurable) explicit knowledge, i.e. skills subject to formal measurement and assessment (Heckman, 2000; Mountford, 1997). The focus on formal qualifications obscures the importance of informal skills and competences which constitute part of total human of capital (Li et al., 1996), and constitute tacit knowledge. Therefore, there is a need to look beyond traditional measures of learning, and to embrace a broader understanding of knowledge" (Baláž et al., 2019: 2).

Recently, researchers have also started talking about "transnational human capital" (Gerhards and Hans, 2013: 102) as "a pool of knowledge and personal competence that allows people to operate in areas other than the nation-state." Naturally, this means that it is also important to consider the components of such capital, including soft skills.

In this book, we would therefore like to go into less-often-considered resources relating to human capital in migration circuits. These include non-certified maker skills, soft skills, mind skills and life skills.

Human capabilities, human capital and migration

Sen pioneered the *capability approach* in which freedom to achieve well-being is in fact what people are able to do and to be, and thus the life they are able to lead (Sen 1979, 2000). Sen highlights the activities humans are able to undertake ("doings") and the types of persons we are able to be ("beings") – they are *capabilities* which are freedoms where people can achieve their potential.

Arguing the differences between human capital and human capabilities, Sen (1997) stated that the approach to real freedoms and capabilities is much broader than the concept of human capital. The latter refers to human skills, knowledge and effort put into obtaining measurable effects of production; human freedoms and capabilities, on the other hand, relate to people's ability to lead what they consider to be valuable lives. The concept of human capital, however, provides a point of reference to understand the essence of human freedoms and possibilities. While the concept of human capital is narrower, the system of human freedoms and opportunities is an integrated socio-economic framework that provides opportunities to establish connections between the two. The paradigm of real freedoms and capabilities offers a much broader perspective on social change than just factors of production.

> Sen's capability approach changes the focus from means (the resources people have and the public goods they can access) to ends (what they are able to do and be with those resources and goods). This shift in focus is justified because resources and goods alone do not ensure that people are able to convert them into actual doings and beings. Two persons with similar sets of goods and resources may nevertheless be able to achieve very different ends depending on their circumstances.[2]

According to Sen (2000) and Nussbaum (2011), human capabilities consist of the answers to the question: what can a person do, what is he/she capable of doing and making, and how can he/she live? Sen (2000) interlinked freedoms and capabilities with a set of mutually interpenetrating opportunities for making choices, taking action and possibilities for what a person is able to achieve in life in a given political, social and economic context. Opportunities are the sum of the internal possibilities of a person and the social, political and economic conditions in which humans choose their own functioning. Sen considers that in the whole set of human opportunities, health and education are the most important.

In her philosophical system, Nussbaum (2011) pointed out that, from a whole set of human capabilities, it is worth focusing on internal capabilities associated with personality traits, intellectual and emotional abilities, and perceptive and physical skills. These are trained and developed in contact with the social, economic, political and family environment. Nussbaum claimed that society should especially promote the development of internal capabilities, but is often responsible for hindering the related capabilities. In Nussbaum's view, while the distinction between related and internal capabilities is not a sharp one, it is important for diagnosing achievements. It also draws attention to basic capabilities that have been developing since birth, while living in a family home, when we gain the basis for developing and educating human capabilities. The functioning of human possibilities is combined with their implementation. Above all, a person can choose available options, which have always been the central analytical axis of economics. If choice is freedom and the exercise of freedoms, then freedom has internal value. The paradigm of human possibilities is not a paradigm about the inner nature of a human. It is a paradigm that asks how human beings are able to develop the ability to do something, taking into account the resources and opportunities that they have under given social, cultural, economic and political conditions.

Sen (2000) stated that some human capabilities are difficult to measure and attempts to find indicators for them can lead to the loss of relevant qualitative information. For this reason, this book uses both quantitative data, and qualitative data that go deep into abilities and try to capture their essence.

The notion of capability was also transposed to migration studies. De Haas (2021) applied capabilities to the developmental side of migration-development interactions as a conceptual redesign of capabilities approach. Certain capabilities are a precondition for large-scale labour migration, he argued, and migration can in turn further expand people's capabilities. De Haas (2014) later combined Carling's aspiration/ability model with Sen's work to establish an "expanded aspirations-capabilities framework" that encompasses bidirectional connections between migration and development. "Capability" and "ability" are essentially synonyms, and they are often used interchangeably in migration research (Dimitriadi, 2017; Randell, 2016). There are slight theoretical differences between the two terms and their associated conceptualisations, however. The aspirations/cap-abilities model is a framework for explaining migration outcomes, while "ability" is simply the component that informs us whether prospective migrants can turn their migration aspirations into moves. The expanded aspirations-capabilities framework includes migration processes as "an intrinsic part of broader processes of social transformation" (De Haas, 2014: 4). "Capabilities" also relate to various components of well-being. The capability to migrate impacts migration outcomes, which may enhance people's capabilities via transfers of financial, human and social capital. (Carling and Schewel, 2018)

> The capabilities approach suggests that the capability to migrate is a valuable freedom in its own right, regardless of people's preferences for staying or leaving. The aspiration model considers "ability" to migrate only among people who aspire to migrate, the "capability" to migrate is relevant to all.
>
> (Carling and Schewel, 2018: 956–957)

The human capabilities approach combined with the aspiration model helps to understand how people fare and act in various conditions and why they choose to migrate or not. It is important to realise what resources, especially those relating to human capital, they are able to mobilise and enhance as a result of their migratory aspirations and actual migratory moves.

Human capacities, human capital and migration

Nussbaum (2011) stated that if a person has abilities, one develops, strengthens and deepens them. The experience of international migration may or may not serve this purpose.

Human capacities are related to human freedoms and capabilities. In the broadest sense, they refer to what a person is capable of in certain social, political and economic conditions, in a given opportunity structure. Human capacities relate to acquiring, absorbing, receiving, and grasping the social world in which an individual is embedded.

Human capacities are human dispositions that have their locus both in the *individual* and *social* types of capacities made from structural, cultural and agential factors (Archer, 2007). Human capacities are socially situated and manifest our thoughts, desires, attitudes, and aspirations; they drive what we do, what we want and do not want to do (Frankfurt, 1971). Therefore they are about being and acting in the social world. Sets of *human capacities* mean that we are radically heterogeneous as subjects, even though we may share objective social positions and have similar social outcomes. The set of human capacities is dynamic, because we modify our goals in terms of their contextual feasibility and our experience of contextual disjuncture. Human capacities are shaped by an "active process of engagement with the world that works through relational reflexivity" (Archer, 2015: 125).

In philosophical terms, Harry G. Frankfurt (1988) claims that human abilities are related to the will of what a person wants to do and what he does not want to do. Human abilities, such as properties, are attributed to man and relate to his and her agency and self-awareness. They are also related to human dispositions, aspirations, attitudes, skills and competences. The latter is especially useful for measuring human capacity in migrant and non-migrant populations.

Human capacities, and especially their acquisition, enhancement and development, as well their transferral, are effects of continuous contact between individual subjective agency and structural conditions (Archer, 2007). In the chapter "Bodies, persons and human enhancement" (Archer, 2018), Margaret Archer discusses two pillars, interrelated human abilities on which social change is built (in Archer's own terms, morphogenesis): *capacity for reflexivity* and *capacity for concern* (the ability to care about one's own life).

Capacity for reflexivity (Archer, 2007, 2018) is preceded by trial and error learning and helps one place oneself in their surrounding context and establish a reflexive relationship with one's environment. Reflexivity is a conversation with oneself, reflection on oneself, internal conversation, one's reactions to structural conditions. Reflexivity gives us the capacity to understand our own potential and our own limitations. We have different types of reflexivity: communicative reflexivity, meta-reflexivity, and autonomous and fractional reflexivity (Archer, 2007). Communicative reflexivity is a constant mirroring in the social eyes of other people, seeking their acceptance and confirmation of one's actions, embedded in social control. Meta-reflexivity is associated with constant criticism of other people's own abilities and abilities. Autonomic reflexivity is associated with self-sufficiency in making decisions and trusting yourself and your own orientation more than other people. We deal with fractional reflexivity when internal conversations bring confusion, distress and uncertainty.

Forms of reflexivity can be practiced by a single person, in the course of life. In migration situations, people practice different types of reflexivity depending on the stage of migration and their circumstances. In the first stage of migration, migrants experience fractional reflexivity, a sense of being lost and confused. They then look for acceptance in the host society and by co-migrants. In the next steps, migrants can develop meta-reflexivity, criticising their own capabilities, how to act in a host society and the capabilities of other migrants and non-migrants. Then, if conditions allow, migrants can develop autonomous reflexivity in decision-making and life orientations, based on one's own abilities and experiences. The reflexivity of migrants gives the opportunity to show how much difference there is between the way people react in structural conditions. Internal conversation can be of particular importance here, because it considers the cognitive and intrapersonal dimensions of informal human capital, which will be discussed later in this book.

The capacity for concern in life (Archer, 2000, 2018) relates to what we want from life, what our life goals are, what our life plan is, what is important to us in life. The decision to migrate is a manifestation of life concern, because people recognise that migration will allow them to achieve better, more effectively defined life goals, to increase their life chances, opportunities and life satisfaction, or simply to prove themselves. These are usually existential concerns relating to the desire to improve the material situation of one's own and the family. Secured material needs can, gradually, turn into intangible concerns relating to ideas, norms, values, competences and skills. The migration context is one of the possible social contexts for achieving life goals.

In his work *What is a person?* Christian Smith (2011: 42–78) refers directly to the human capacities which constitute a human. He attempts to catalogue them, offering detailed categories. He focuses primarily on human abilities that cause changes in the social world, both material and immaterial. Smith divides human capacities into: (1) *existence capacities,* connected with self-consciousness; (2) *primary experience capacities,* connected with experiencing the world; (3) *secondary experience capacities,* connected with social memory and emotional experience; (4) *creative capacities,* connected with reflexivity, forming identity, communicating meanings, creating and using technologies, and introducing actions and interactions; (5) *higher order capacities* connected with humanism and abstract thinking.

Human capacities do not occur singly; they combine into bundles. Capacities develop and strengthen through interactions and relationships between people. They are socially oriented. They are practiced not to maintain isolated individuals, but to make people create relationships with each other (Donati and Archer, 2015). Although one thinks about the human abilities of a single person, one must always remember that they are socially rooted and shaped and perform social functions related to building relationships between people (Smith, 2011).

The concept of human capacities is helpful in considering human capital with a special focus on the human rather than the capital factor. In the migratory context, we treat the human as an agent-creator, maintainer and user of knowledge and skills (Armstrong, 2006; Archer, 2007) that are relevant for the reinforcement of human capital. People with their agency acquire but also enhance knowledge, skill, competency, capacity and experience (Kwon, 2009).

Human capacities conflate two domains: the individual domain, consisting of cognitive and intrapersonal components, and the social domain, consisting of interpersonal components (c.f. National Research Council, 2012). The individual domain relates to the cognitive aspects of reasoning, knowledge and creativity, which also involves critical thinking, information literacy, argumentation and innovation, as well as to the intrapersonal capacity to manage one's emotions and behaviours to achieve goals, including learning; it also relates to flexibility, initiative, appreciation for diversity and reflexivity. The social domain covers more interpersonal and relational aspects of expressing ideas, interpreting and responding to messages from others, and also involves communication, collaboration, responsibility and conflict resolution. (cf. Grabowska and Jastrzebowska, 2019).

The concept of human capacities has just been introduced to migration studies (cf. Grabowska and Jastrzebowska, 2019; Grabowska, 2019) and relates mostly to becoming, being and acting in a socially mobile world. Both individual and social human capacities can be affected by migration; the capacity for reflexivity and capacity for concern about life, especially, gain new importance in migratory contexts. International migration is not the be-all and end-all of the acquisition and enhancement of human capacities, but can create significant non-formal social learning situations that clear the way for new non-material components of informal human capital (Grabowska and Jastrzebowska, 2019).

Psychological Capital, human capital and migration

Psychological Capital (PsyCap) comprises four primary psychological resources from positive psychology: self-efficacy, hope, optimism and resilience (cf. Newman et al., 2014). PsyCap concerns "who you are" and "who you are becoming" (Luthans, Avey, Avolio, Norman and Combs, 2006; Luthans and Youssef, 2004). However, in psychological literature, PsyCap is distinguished from human and social capital (cf. Newman et al., 2016), and has been mostly discussed from the perspective of organisations, employee outcomes and employees' efficiency. PsyCap has the potential to be developed through training and intentional practice (Luthans, 2012; Luthans, Avey, Clapp-Smith and Li, 2008). In this book we would like to juxtapose PsyCap with human capital and social capital.

Self-efficacy refers to a person's confidence in their ability to mobilise motivation, cognitive resources and courses of action in order to achieve high levels of performance (Stajkovic and Luthans, 1998). People with a high level of self-efficacy generally have a stronger belief in their ability to control outcomes and succeed in addressing difficult challenges than those people with low self-efficacy (Bandura, 1977, 1982).

Hope has two components: agency and pathways (Snyder et al., 1996). Agency refers to an individual's motivation to succeed at a specific task in a context, while pathways concern the method or means by which that task may be accomplished (Luthans, Norman, Avolio, and Avey, 2006). Individuals with high levels of hope show greater agency and are more likely to exhibit the capacity to develop alternative pathways to accomplish their goals (Luthans, et al., 2006).

Optimism refers to an individual's expectancy of positive outcomes (Scheier, Carver, and Bridges, 2001). People with high optimism generally build positive expectancies that motivate them to pursue their goals and deal with difficult situations (Seligman, 1998).

Resilience refers to an individual's ability to bounce back from adversity, uncertainty, risk or failure, and to adapt to changing and stressful life demands (Masten and Reed, 2002; Tugade and Fredrickson, 2004). Individuals with high resilience tend to be better at adapting in the face of negative experiences and changes in the external environment (Luthans, Vogelgesang, and Lester, 2006).

PsyCap might be of greater benefit to minority groups in the workplace, such as migrant workers, given that it will provide them with the confidence to seek much-needed support and advice from others in the workplace (Combs et al., 2012).

To sum up, broadly speaking, PsyCap represents an individual's growth and development, comprising four aspects: (a) being able to face a challenge (self-efficacy) (b) having positive attitudes towards present and future success (optimism), (c) being able to adjust paths to success (hope), (d) being able to recover and move on when faced with problems (resilience).

PsyCap has considered migration to a very limited extent,[3] mostly in order to find the ways how to support refugees (cf. Newman et al., 2016). A few studies also examined the factors that affect the psychological wellbeing of voluntary migrants (Jasinskaja-Lahti et al., 2006). Jasinskaja-Lahti et al. (2006) found that strong social support networks were directly related to voluntary migrants' psychological wellbeing, and buffered the negative effects of perceived discrimination. Colic-Peisker (2009) and Fozdar and Torezani (2008) found that social support predicted refugees' psychological wellbeing, and Young (2001) also found that social support mitigated the negative effects of stress among refugees.

In their research on migration, knowledge and competences, Janta et al. (2019) indirectly referred to PsyCap by including the concept of "bouncing back when faced with adversity", which is an element of resilience acquired by migrants through their migratory experience.

PsyCap is also indirectly referenced in studies on youth mobile transitions (Robertson, Harris and Baldassar, 2018) where self-efficacy and resilience were mentioned as resources that young migrants could obtain on their path towards independence and adulthood.

In this book, PsyCap refers to human capacities. It is particularly connected to the capacity for reflexivity, which concerns intrapersonal aspects of informal human capital relating to internal conversations, autonomy in activities, setting and striving towards goals, taking one's life into one's own hands.

Conservation of resources, human capital and migration

Hobfoll (1989) offered *Conservation of Resources Theory* (COR) which is about motivation which facilitates humans to maintain the current resources and to acquire new ones (cf. Jastrzebowska, 2020). It is connected with PsyCap. Hobfoll distinguished four kinds of resources: objects, conditions, personal characteristics and energy. Usually COR was discussed in relation to stress. For the purpose of this book we discuss COR in reference to international migration which might both create and cope with stress, namely building up resilience.

Objects as a resource are rare items which are worth possessing. Values are attached to them. They might also increase social status. For instance, a home – property has a value, emotional and economic. In terms of human capital object resources might relate to diplomas, certificates, equipment etc. International migration can help to acquire them.

Conditions are resources that they are valued after some time. They relate for instance to marriage, tenured job, seniority. International migration creates conditions by itself usually for better paid jobs, employability, acquisition of new skills, new life opportunities for mating and networking.

Personal characteristics as resources mostly relate to one's mind-set, an opening towards the world and seeing events as a predictable sequence. They are connected to personal traits and skills. Their maintenance is connected with increasing self-esteem and supporting a positive meaning of self. They are clearly connected with an individual, intra-relational human capital. International migration might facilitate an opening up of minds (Grabowska, 2019) and self-confidence, especially among young migrant adults (cf. Grabowska and Jastrzebowska, 2019).

Energies are the fourth and last resource category offered by Hobfoll and include knowledge, time and money. "These resources are typified not by their intrinsic value so much as their value in aiding the acquisition of other kinds of resources" (Hobfoll, 1998: 517). They are very important in the context of an acquisition of human capital in migratory circumstances because they are connected with a power to act – to have a motivation and a strength in decision making and risk international migration actively searching for socio-cultural situations which can enrich us, e.g. exercising a foreign language competence, networking and making deeper relations.

Resources can be lost, gained, invested, replaced, maintained, appraised, evaluated and devalued. International migration might create opportunities for all the processes mentioned in the previous sentence thus while migrating people mostly focus on what they might gain instead of what they might lose. Consideration of distance from home and parental family also helps to evaluate resources. International migration can create conditions for both investment and devaluation of resources. It depends on the job sector, type of contract, job-competence fit (cf. Jastrzebowska, 2020), job place description and workplace relationality – in other words to what extent a person can learn by observing, communicating and doing.

To sum up, resources have both subjective and objective components. The field of migration can benefit from studying resources especially in light of drain-gain-circulation discussions. Resources and their conservation/maintenance can help to conceptualise and operationalise informal human capital.

Tacit knowledge, human capital and migration

Not all knowledge is explicit knowledge; there is also tacit knowledge, which is an important resource in its own right.

> By knowledge we refer to the acquisition of principles, concepts, theories, words, rules, procedures and techniques; it is the result of a learning process that can be formal or informal and can be certified or uncertified. When the knowledge is formally acquired and certified, we define it as explicit. By skill we mean the capacity to use the knowledge in specific contexts in order to generate solutions to problems or develop creative solutions. By competence we mean the capacity to use knowledge and skills in complex situations.
>
> (Staniscia et al., 2019)

The concept of tacit knowledge has been used by Williams and Baláž (2005) with regards to human capital and was introduced by Polanyi (1958, 1966). Polanyi (1966: 7) argues that "all knowledge is either tacit or rooted in tacit knowledge. A wholly explicit knowledge is unthinkable". A person's tacit knowledge comprises what they know without being able to understand or explain the processes lying behind (cf. Lulle, Janta, and Emilsson, 2019).

The skills and competences acquired in the course of international migration can incorporate and reinforce tacit knowledge, in addition to explicit knowledge (cf. Polanyi, 1958, 1966; Williams and Baláž, 2008a, 2008b). Tacit knowledge is intangible and can be acquired and developed not only through formal education and training, but also through learning-by-observing, learning-by-communicating and learning-by-doing in migratory situations (Grabowska, 2018).

> Tacit knowledge is a form of awareness that, at first, is only usable by the individual, although it can be transferred to others. In contrast, codified knowledge can be communicated by symbols and language and is commodifiable. The two are inseparable, however, tacit knowledge is almost always required to unlock codified knowledge; moreover, competitive advantage is normally the outcome of how they are combined. (…) Human mobility is critical in this, with individuals performing the roles of specific knowledge carriers.
>
> (Williams, Baláž, and Wallace, 2004: 30–31)

Of course, as Williams and Baláž emphasise in various publications, some skill and competence sets are time, space and cultural context specific. They are therefore not always transferable between origin and destination and upon return. Fortunately, there are many skills that are transferable, constituting a kind of "global skill set" in which intangible tacit knowledge can be encapsulated through practice, throughout the course of migration and upon return (cf. Palovic, Janta and Williams 2019).

In their migration studies, Williams and Baláž (2005; Baláž and Williams, 2004) introduced and tested a five-component competence model formulated by Evans and Rainbird (2002: 88–89), which includes both transferable and non-transferable competences.

> "Content-related and practical competences (e.g., willingness to carry out a variety of duties); Competences related to attitudes and values (e.g., responsibility or reliability); Learning competences (e.g., openness to learning or perceptiveness); Methodological competencies (e.g., networking skills or ability to handle multiple tasks); and Social and interpersonal competencies (e.g., communication skills or awareness of others' viewpoints).
>
> (Williams and Baláž, 2005: 444)

This means that learning in migratory settings brings effects of transferable components of the competences listed by Evans and Rainbird (2002). Williams and Baláž (2005) argue that some of these competences, such as flexibility and openness to new ideas, are more effectively enhanced abroad than at home. Migrants develop skills to create networks and networking both to organise work and accommodation and to adapt and finally to build trust and cooperation in teams. Successful migration also helps to develop self-confidence, especially when this is combined with social recognition which helps to valorise skills. Social recognition of skills strengthened by a migratory experience helps in effective communication and self-confidence and it is negotiable. Social recognition relates to social expectations and internationally mobile persons can challenge how they and their knowledge and skills (both explicit and tacit) are recognised in various contexts, organisations and workplaces.

> (…) it is important to understand better how individuals harness and use tacit forms of key competences as they move between roles and settings. (…) This dictum is even more pertinent when considering the transfer of competencies, embodied in individual migrants, between places and jobs.
>
> (Williams and Baláž, 2005: 446)

Recent studies by Baláž et al. (2019), Staniscia et al. (2019) and McGarry et al. (2019) have advanced our understanding of human capital in relation to tacit knowledge which can be transferred upon migrants' return.

> The transfer of tacit knowledge is most effectively realised via human mobility which enables face-to-face exchanges, or direct observation. Tacit knowledge is considered more valuable than explicit knowledge because of the costs of mobility / migration, and also because it is difficult to imitate.
>
> (Baláž et al., 2019: 3)

Baláž et al. (2019) conceptualise the skills and competences acquired by migrants from the perspective of the tacit and explicit knowledge in the course of migration. In their study, Baláž et al. tested how valuable the experiences abroad of people had been in terms of the following factors: (1) acquiring formal qualifications; (2) learning new skills; (3) the ability to deal with new challenges; (4) self-confidence; (5) learning new languages; and (6) learning to adapt to new cultures. Especially points on abilities with dealing with new situations, self-confidence and adaptation relate clearly to the above discussed PsyCap.

Staniscia et al. (2019) showed that an important component of knowledge and the human capital formation of young migrants is learning or mastering a language (based on their case of Southern Europeans). The acquisition of language capital is related to the duration of the stay abroad and the primary reasons for migration. Migrants who have a return strategy invest less in language learning (Dustmann, 1999; see also Lulle, Janta, and Emilsson, 2019). Lulle et al.'s study also considered soft elements of human capital: the development of self-identity, self-construction, self-recognition and self-esteem, self-confidence, flexibility, resilience, adaptability, communication skills, risk tolerance and the construction of an international social capital.

McGarry et al. (2019) take into account two key concepts of human capital and well-being. They argue that tacit competencies, defined as skills, ideas and experiences that people acquire and enhance but are not codified, are especially valued by circular migrants as facilitators of multiple migratory processes and are of importance to levels of life satisfaction among young circular migrants.

Therefore every migrant is a learner, a knowledge carrier and a knowledge creator, especially of tacit knowledge, overcoming the dichotomy between unskilled and skilled migrants (cf. Robinson and Carey, 2000; Hagan et al., 2015). This is a crucial argument in this book, as its central argument about the impact of international migration on informal components of human capital is based on both skilled and unskilled migrants, including skilled migrants doing unskilled jobs as well as formally unskilled migrants doing jobs demanding specific skills.

Total human capital and migration

In order not to omit what has been already established in the literature on human capital on both formal and informal ends, it is necessary to consider a comprehensive approach, namely that of total human capital. Due to the various difficulties involved in measuring intangible, informal components of human capital, analysts and researchers have mostly focused on clear and easy-to-measure proxies relating to education or years of schooling validated through diplomas, degrees and certificates which act as proof of qualifications and work experience. They relate to occupational position and income. Migration researchers called for holistic research and measurements of total human capital (Li et al., 1996; Findlay et al., 1996; Williams and Baláž, 2005; Williams and Baláž, 2008a; Hagan et al., 2015), covering both explicit and tacit capital and both its formal and its informal components, as it is otherwise too easy to classify migrants as wasting and experiencing "brain-drain" and they do not transfer knowledge and skills if they worked in low or medium-skilled jobs abroad. Proxies of tacit components of human capital are more difficult to identify and to measure than proxies of explicit human capital. They originate from tacit knowledge (Polanyi, 1966), which was discussed in the previous subsection, and relate to soft skills which are transferable across international contexts. Total human capital covers various aspects of acquisition linked to migration: explicit and tacit knowledge such as a foreign language spoken in a host country, codified and certified and soft, formal and informal qualifications and social and relational capacities (Lulle, Janta, and Emilsson, 2019).

Hagan et al. (2015) conceptualise the acquisition of non-certified and non-validated technical and manual skills as well as soft skills as "lifelong human capital formation" to encompass both formal and informal learning along the life course path (cf. Wassink, 2020: 5–6).

Reich (1992) identifies three categories of tacit skills: technical (involving high levels of symbolic manipulation), routine (repetitive work), and social (which facilitate communication and social interaction) (cf. Williams and Baláž, 2005: 444).

> (...) Hence, interpersonal skills, confidence, the role of social recognition and the different forms of knowledge that stem from the migration experience itself – all need to be incorporated into research on human capital dynamics in the context of migration.
>
> (cf. Lulle et al., 2018: 5)

Total human capital represents the catalogue of soft skills, such as interpersonal abilities, confidence, and communication (Li et al., 1996; Williams and Baláž, 2005). Hagan et al. (2015) also include non-validated and non-certified technical and manual skills, arguing that acquiring technical and social competences through interaction and observation, the totality of migratory-enhanced "total human capital" may bring more labour market opportunities upon return even for low-skilled migrants than before migration (Hagan, Demonsant, and Chávez, 2014: 1; Hagan and Wassink, 2016).

> Even where individuals have what are socially constructed as unskilled jobs abroad, these may provide opportunities to enhance human capital through acquiring (foreign) language and interpersonal skills, or non-workplace education and training. This broader array of skills is captured in the notion of total human capital (Li et al., 1996) although it is essential to consider how this is valorised in particular spaces through a set of social relationships.
>
> (Williams, Baláž, and Wallace, 2004: 31)

Williams and Baláž (2008a: 18) in their monograph *International Migration and Knowledge* conceptualise a systematic theoretical perspective in line with the total human capital approach: from human capital to knowledge(s). They differentiate three groups of skills: symbolic, technical and social which contribute to competences and therefore to codified and tacit knowledge which can be embrained, embodied, embedded and encultured; the whole process takes into account the economic environment linked to knowledge management, e.g. in Central Europe.

McGarry et al. (2019) highlight the challenges faced by migrants in Europe in mobilising and maximising human capital. Measures of human capital based on qualifications or occupational status fail to account for the problems experienced by migrants in contemporary labour markets (Csedő, 2008). The total human capital is crucial to the effective communication and transposition of formal qualifications and professional experiences across international borders (Williams and Baláž, 2005). People primarily acquire non-occupationally specific skills through migration, which are hard to measure.

Life and job satisfaction, human capital and migration

Adding life and job satisfaction to the concepts discussed above will help to formulate migratory-impacted informal human capital in a comprehensive and multidimensional way that also goes beyond the traditional definition of health. The arguments presented in this book require three dimensions of wellbeing: social, economic and personal/ psychological.

> Psychological [personal] wellbeing is defined as an individual's cognitive assessment of satisfaction with his/her life circumstances.
>
> (Diener et al., 1985)

> There is growing recognition that although psychological wellbeing is relatively stable over time, it can be influenced by contextual factors such as the provision of social support from others in one's social networks.
>
> (e.g. Daniels and Guppy, 1994; Gallagher and Vella-Brodrick, 2008; Siedlecki et al., 2014; cf. Newman et al., 2017).

The Five Ways to Wellbeing were developed by the New Economics Foundation (NEF) on behalf of the Foresight Commission in the UK and adapted for New Zealand by the Mental Health Foundation. The Five Ways to Wellbeing are: connect, be active, keep learning, give, and take notice. The National Wellness Institute promotes six dimensions of wellness: emotional, occupational, physical, social, intellectual, and spiritual.

Through international mobility, people strive to better their lives in many areas, which covers the three above-mentioned dimensions of well-being: personal, social and economic. The betterment of life needs also to be extended into freedom, including freedom of movement, also for work, civic liberties, and a clean environment. To better human life is in line with the capability approach as defined by Sen, which was discussed earlier in this chapter. For the purpose of this analysis we may say that economic well-being is connected with job performance, lifestyle, social status, including migrants' situations after return. Social well-being encompasses inter-personal support and social ties. Psychological well-being relates to self-efficacy, optimism, hope and resilience which stand out for PsyCap.

In a seminal study titled *The Well-being of Nations,* published in 2001, the OECD included well-being in the definition of human capital, thereby asserting a causal relation between various components of the human capital that resides in people and the creation of well-being.

> The knowledge, skills, competencies and attributes embodied in individuals that facilitate the creation of personal, social and economic well-being.
>
> (OECD, 2005: 18)

McGarry et al. (2019) claim that resources of human capital relate also to life satisfaction. They conclude that "human capital portfolios of migrants are constructed in tandem with life course development and play a crucial role in determining life satisfaction outcomes" (McGarry et al., 2019: 5).

As Hendriks and Bartram (2019) point out, subjective well-being could be a way to measure migration outcomes. Well-being should be measured as a comprehensive indicator that includes a variety of life domains, primarily self-assessment criteria of life satisfaction[4] and their effects. A sense of well-being allows individuals to evaluate the importance of different aspects of life, including an experience of international migration. The literature of well-being widely recognised that life satisfaction varies across individuals, and that even for a single individual, it is influenced by time and space. Subjective measures of well-being may be more effective than objective measures of outcomes, because they take into account different personal aspirations and expectations. Subjective components of well-being raise awareness of the limitations of objective indicators in evaluating individual and societal well-being (Bache, 2019; cf. Ambrosetti and Paprusso, 2021).

Migration-Impacted Informal Human Capital (MigCap)

Based on the legacies of the above-mentioned concepts, we will develop the concept of Migration-Impacted Informal Human Capital (MigCap) necessary for the subsequent methodological and empirical steps of this book. Before that, however, we will summarise the essentials of the various concepts mentioned on the previous pages in the table below (Table 2.1).

Migration-Impacted Informal Human Capital (MigCap) is illustrated in a four-component model, presented later (Figure 2.1). The cube design reflects the interplay between informally learned mind skills or cognitive skills, soft skills or personal and people skills, maker skills or non-certified and non-validated technical and manual skills and life skills meaning well-being connected to life and job satisfaction. The shape of the four-dimensional cube formulates multiple facets, dynamism and interconnectedness (see Figure 2.1) of informal human capital. Migration processes, migration dynamics and migratory situations are also featured in the model. Due to migration, people change contexts, opportunity structures and environments to better accumulate and maximise resources (cf. Hagan et al., 2015). The MigCap approach allows us to distinguish between the *intrinsic* and the *instrumental* value of international migration's impact on human capital. The instrumental value consists of financial and material benefits, while the intrinsic value concerns self-development, independence, experience (Carling and Schewel, 2018), agency, reflexivity, self-efficacy, resilience, optimism, life and job satisfaction, and intrapersonal and interpersonal communication.

Both the dynamics and the mechanisms through which MigCap yields individual-level outcomes of mind skills, maker skills, soft skills and life skills, are crucial to this analysis.

Informal human capital can be acquired and transferred between social spaces. The processes of acquisition, transferral, application and obstruction of informal human capital are embedded in social and cultural contexts, relations, practices and local labour markets (cf. Hagan et al., 2015). Migrants are context filters.

MigCap can be transferred between people located in different countries. For example a returnee can bring back MigCap to an organisation or local community in a country of origin. Therefore the conceptual model should also include the stages which forgo the transfer of MigCap. First stage concerns the exposure to opportunities, social situations in which MigCap can be acquired and developed. Then if opportunities appear and a migrant is able to take an advantage out of them, she or he can acquire new components of MigCap or develop and enhance the existing ones.

Table 2.1 An overview of the discussed conceptual frameworks

Approach and leading authors	Key characteristics
Human capital (Mincer, 1958; Schultz, 1961; Becker, 1962)	Human capital relates to knowledge, qualifications, attitudes, capabilities, motivations, health, experience and skills. It is predominately measured by formally certified knowledge and qualifications, and relates mainly to obtaining measurable production outcomes in relation to production power and their impact on the economy.
Human capabilities (Sen, 2000; Nussbaum, 2011)	Human capabilities form a socio-economic system which is much wider than the concept of human capital. Human capabilities relate to the ability to run a good life and to strengthen one's own freedoms and opportunities for making choices. Human capabilities consider what a person can do and what he is able to do in given social, political, cultural and economic circumstances; they inform us how people can develop the capability to make life in given structural conditions.
Psychological Capital (PsyCap) (Luthans and Youssef, 2007; Luthans, Youssef, and Avolio, 2007)	Psychological Capital (PsyCap) consists of four primary psychological resources from positive psychology: self-efficacy, hope, optimism and resilience. It is concerned with "who you are" and "who are you becoming".
Conservation of resources (COR) (Hobfoll, 1989)	Conservation of resources is about motivation which facilitates humans to maintain the current resources and to acquire new ones. There are four kinds of resources: objects, conditions, personal characteristics and energy.
Human capacities (Frankfurt, 1988; Archer, 2018; Smith, 2015; Donati and Archer, 2015; cf. Grabowska and Jastrzebowska, 2019; Grabowska, 2019)	Human capacities are formed on the constant interplay of individual agency and structural circumstances on three levels: lifelong and life-wide learning, corrections of behaviours, and adaptability. Capacities can be divided into two broad ontological categories: capacity for reflexivity – how people react to structural conditions, and capacity for life concerns – what we want and do not want from life, what our goals are, what we consider important in life. Human capacities do not occur independently, but exist in what one might term "bundles".
Life and job satisfaction (Diener et al., 1985; Newman et al., 2017; OECD, 2001)	The ability of an individual reflected through self-assessment of life satisfaction, which includes job satisfaction. It covers three dimensions: economic, social and personal/psychological, and includes decisions and actions aimed at achieving a normal, good life.

Approach and leading authors	Key characteristics
Tacit knowledge *Tacit forms of competences* (Williams and Baláž, 2005)	Tacit knowledge is an individual's awareness of how to unlock codified knowledge in a given social situation and circumstances. It can be transferred to others. Tacit knowledge helps to harness tacit forms of competences relating to content and practice, values and attitudes, learning, networking and multi-tasking.
Total Human Capital (Li et al. 1996; Findlay et al. 1996; Hagan and Wissink 2020)	Total Human Capital relates to formally certified and validated knowledge and skills as well as non-certified and non-validated knowledge and skills; it highlights that both formal and informal resources are crucial for human development, communicating and seeing others' point of view.

Source: own elaboration, see also Grabowska (2019).

The transfer happens though human carriers and in opportunity structures where MigCap can be applied.

When there are no opportunities to be applied, MigCap it can be muted, put on hold till the moment new opportunities appear. Sometimes migrants actively search for new opportunities or create them for their own sake and their environments.

Intended or unintended acquisition and enhancement of informal human capital at every dimension can be seen as a form of agency while the contexts, situations, environments to which migrants are exposed, which

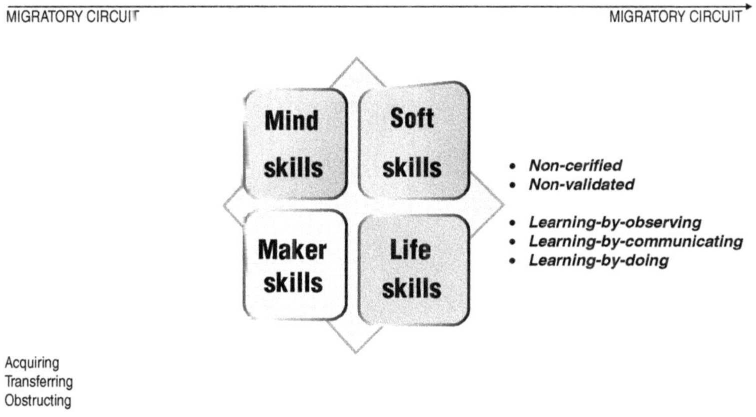

MIGRATORY CIRCUIT   MIGRATORY CIRCUIT

Mind skills   **Soft skills**

Maker skills   **Life skills**

- *Non-certified*
- *Non-validated*

- *Learning-by-observing*
- *Learning-by-communicating*
- *Learning-by-doing*

Acquiring
Transferring
Obstructing

Figure 2.1 Four-component model of MigCap
Source: Author's elaboration.

they encounter and in what they are embedded form structural opportunities and limitations.

As MigCap is informal, its components are non-certified and non-validated. They can be acquired, developed and enhanced through learning-by-observing, learning-by-communicating and learning-by-doing (cf. Grabowska, 2018).

Each component of the MigCap model is embedded and conceptually justified by various theoretical approaches analysed in the first part of this chapter (see Figure 2.2). Informal human capital conceives both mind skills, hand skills and soft skills. Tacit knowledge and competences enclose mind skills and soft skills. Being and acting in the social world in given circumstances grasps various types of soft skills. Then capacity for reflexivity strongly connects with soft skills and capacity for life concern. Psychological capital (PsyCap) comprehends various types of soft skills and various dimensions of life concerns.

The concepts of knowledge, skills, abilities and competences are sometimes used interchangeably, generating confusion in the literature (Williams and Baláž 2008a). In this book we deliberately use the single concept of skills as learned abilities to be in a society and to perform an action. It is also an ability to apply information, know-how, know-when, know-why.

Some key skills and personal attributes relevant to human capital may be categorised as follows: 1. Communication (including foreign language

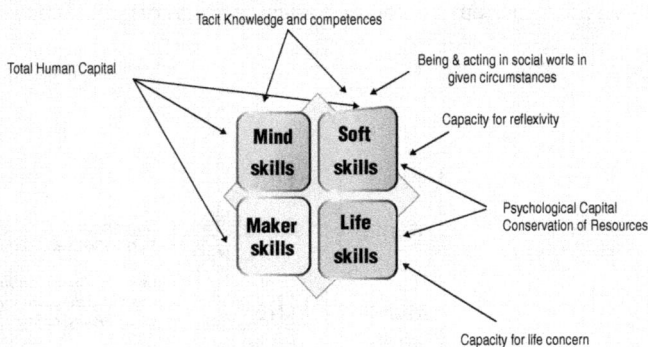

Figure 2.2 The conceptual map and interplays between concepts constituting the MigCap
Source: Author's elaboration.

competence in each of the items directly below) – Listening – Speaking – Reading – Writing 2. Numeracy 3. Intra-personal skills – Motivation/ perseverance – "Learning to learn" and self-discipline (including self-directed learning strategies) – Capacity to make judgements based on a relevant set of ethical values and goals in life 4. Inter-personal skills – Teamwork – Leadership 5. Other skills and attributes (relevant to many areas above) – Facility in using information and communications technology – Tacit knowledge – Problem-solving (also embedded in other types of skills) – Physical attributes and dexterity.

(OECD, 2005: 18)

Mind skills or cognitive skills relate to working knowledge learned informally through observing, communicating and doing. Therefore they are connected to the capacity to learn in social situations. Migratory situations amplify tacit knowledge accumulation due to novelties of socio-cultural situations.

Personal and people skills are commonly known as soft skills. They refer to the internal capacity for reflexivity: moderating and editing own behaviours, expressions, judgements, world look, mind-set and capacity for concerns and reflection on practical experience gained abroad. People skills reflect social, interpersonal capacity for relational agency. Relational agency is defined as:

> a temporal embedded process of social engagement, informed by the past (habitual aspect), but also oriented toward the future (as a capacity to imagine alternative possibilities) and toward the present (as a capacity to contextualise past habits and future projects with the contingencies of the moment).
>
> (Emirbayer and Mische, 1998: 963)

Maker skills or manual, technical skills are non-validated, non-certified and acquired usually on a site They relate to using hands in a skilful and coordinated way to grasp and manipulate machines, various construction techniques but also production line and agricultural works.

Life skills conceive life satisfaction and job satisfaction while seeking a normal, good life by migrants.

Below we define the MigCap.

Box 2.1 MigCap (Migration-Impacted Informal Human Capital)

MigCap is an intangible multicomponent human resource comprising mind skills, soft skills, maker skills and life skills. It predominantly consists of tacit skills, though it also includes a number of explicit skills. MigCap is a non-validated, non-codified and non-certified human asset. It is dynamic; as such, it can be shaped throughout a course of migration. It can be acquired, developed, enhanced, mobilised, maximised, transferred, recognised, applied, utilised. It is migration-dependent in terms of type of migration, duration of migration, place of residence, job character and workplace environment. It may be affected by age/ birth cohort, gender, education, personality traits and destination country. Not only means of MigCap are important resources and their conservation or maintenance but also ends – what people are going to do with them.

Source: Author's elaboration.

In the empirical sections of this book we will be demonstrating and testing various interplays between the four components of the MigCap model: mind skills, soft skills, maker skills and life skills in various geographical and socio-cultural contexts for migrants from Central Europe and Mexico.

Notes

1 https://openknowledge.worldbank.org/handle/10986/30498 (accessed 20/12/2020).
2 https://plato.stanford.edu/entries/capability-approach/ (accessed 20/12/2020).
3 Also, resilience and vulnerability are key concepts of the ongoing EU-funded project on the integration of migrant youths from non-EU countries: MIMY (www.mimy.eu), in which the author of this book participates.
4 Global assessment of a person's quality of life according to her chosen criteria.

References

Ambrosetti, E. and Paparusso, A. (2020). What are the Main Factors Associated with Immigrants' Subjective Well-being in Italy? Evidence from Self-reported Life Satisfaction. *International Migration.* doi:10.1111/imig.12780.

Anacka, M. and Fihel, A. (2012). Selektywność emigracji i migracji powrotnych Polaków – o procesie „wypłukiwania". *Central and Eastern European Migration Review,* 1(1), 57–67.

Archer, M. S. (2007). *Making our Way through the World: Human Reflexivity and Social Mobility.* Cambridge: Cambridge University Press.

Archer, M. S. (2015). Socialization as relational reflexivity. In: P. Donati and M.S. Archer (ed.), *Relational Subject* (123–154). Cambridge: Cambridge University Press.

Archer, M. S. (2018). Bodies, persons and human enhancement: Why these distinctions matter. In I. Al-Amoudi and M. Morgan (ed.), *Realist Responses to Post-Human Society: Ex Machina* (20–42). London: Routledge.

Arif, G. M. and Irfan. M. (1997). Return migration and occupational change: The case of Pakistani migrants returned from the Middle East. *The Pakistan Development Peview*, 36(1), 1–37.

Armstrong, M. (2006). *Strategic Human Resource Management-A Guide to Action*, 3rd Ed. London: Kogan Page.

Bache, C. (2019). Challenges to economic integration and social Inclusion of Syrian refugees in Turkey. *Career Development International*, 25(1), 14–18.

Baláž, V. and Williams, A. M. (2004). "Been there, done that": International student migration and human capital transfers from the UK to Slovakia. *Population, Space and Place*, 10(3), 217–237.

Baláž, V., Williams, A. M., Moravčíková, K., and Chrančoková, M. (2019). What competences, which migrants? Tacit and explicit knowledge acquired via migration. *Journal of Ethnic and Migration Studies*, 47(8), 1758–1774.

Bandura, A. (1977). Self-efficacy: toward a unifying theory of behavioural change. *Psychological Review*, 84(2): 191–215.

Bandura, A. (1982). Self-efficacy mechanism in human agency. *American psychologist*, 37(2), 122.

Barrett, A. and O'Connell, O. (2001). Is there a wage premium for returning Irish migrants? IZA Discussion Paper Series No. 135.

Becker, G. S. (1962). Investment in human capital: A theoretical analysis. *Journal of Political Economy*, 70(5), 9–49.

Becker, G. S. (1993). *Human capital: A theoretical and empirical analysis, with special reference to education*. Chicago: University of Chicago Press.

Becker, G. S. (1994). *Human capital revisited. W: Human Capital: A Theoretical and Empirical Analysis with Special Reference to Education*. Chicago: University of Chicago Press.

Borjas, G. J. (2000) Ethnic enclaves and assimilation. *Swedish Economic Policy Review*, 7(2), 89–122.

Bourdieu, P. (1986). The Forms of Capital. In J. G. Richardson (ed.), *Handbook of Theory and Research for Sociology of Education*. London: Greenwood Press.

Brickell, K. and Datta, A. (Eds.). (2011). *Translocal geographies*. Ashgate Publishing, Ltd.

Carletto, C. and Kilic, T. (2011) Moving up the ladder? The impact of migration experience on occupational mobility in Albania. *The Journal of Development Studies*, 47(6), 846–869.

Carling, J. and Schewel, K. (2013). Revisiting aspiration and ability in international migration. *Journal of Ethnic and Migration Studies*, 44(6), 945–963.

Chiswick, B. (1999). Are immigrants favourably self-selected? *American Economic Review*, 89(2), 181–185.

Chiswick, B. R. and Miller P. W. (2003). The complementarity of language and other human capital: Immigrant earnings in Canada. *Economics of Education Review*, 22(5), 469–480.

Chiswick, B. R. and Miller, P. W. (2012). Negative and positive assimilation, skill transferability, and linguistic distance. *Journal of Human Capital*, 6(1), 35–55.

Colic-Peisker, V. (2009). Visibility, settlement success and life satisfaction in three refugee communities in Australia. *Ethnicities*, 9(2), 175–199.

Combs, G. M., Milosevic, I., Jeung, W., and Griffith J. (2012). Ethnic identity and job attribute preferences: The role of collectivism and psychological capital. *Journal of Leadership and Organization Studies*, 19, 5–16.

Csedő, K. (2008). Negotiating skills in the global city: Hungarian and Romanian professionals and graduates in London. *Journal of Ethnic and Migration Studies*, 34(5), 803–823.

D'Aubeterre Buznego, M. E. (2012). Empezar de nuevo: migración femenina a Estados Unidos. Retornos y reinserción en la Sierra Norte de Puebla, México. *Norteamérica*, 7(1), 149–180.

Daniels, K., Guppy, A. (1994). Relationships between aspects of work-related psychological well-being. *The Journal of Psychology*, 128(6), 691–694.

De Haas, H. (2005). International migration, remittances and development: myths and facts. *Third World Quarterly*, 26(8), 1269–1284.

De Haas, H. and Rodríguez, F. (2010). Mobility and human development: introduction. *Journal of Human Development and Capabilities*, 11(2), 177–184.

De Haas, H. (2014). Migration theory: Quo vadis? Working Paper 100, University of Oxford, https://ora.ox.ac.uk/objects/uuid:45aacf94-8f24-4294-9c74-cbc8453fcbfb.

De Haas, H. (2021). A theory of migration: the aspirations-capabilities framework. *Comparative Migration Studies*, 9(1), 1–35.

Demerouti, E., van Eeuwijk, E., Snelder, M., and Wild, U. (2011). Assessing the effects of a "personal effectiveness" training on psychological capital, assertiveness and self-awareness using self-other agreement. *Career Development International*, 16, 60–81.

Diener, E., Emmons, R. A., Larsen, R. J., and Griffin, S. (1985). The Satisfaction with Life Scale. *Journal of Personality Assessment*, 49(1), 71–75.

Dimitriadi, A. (2017). In search of asylum: Afghan migrants in Greece. *European Journal of Migration and Law*, 19(1), 57–76.

Donati, P. and Archer, M. S. (2015). *The Relational Subject*. Cambridge: Cambridge University Press.

Dustmann, C. (1999). Temporary migration, human capital, and language fluency of migrants. *The Scandinavian Journal of Economics*, 101(2), 297–314.

Dustmann, C. and Kirchkamp, O. (2002). The optimal migration duration and activity choice after re-migration. *Journal of Development Economics*, 67(2), 351–372.

Emirbayer, M. and Mische, A. (1998). What is agency? *American Journal of Sociology*, 103(4), 962–1023.

European Centre for the Development of Vocational Training (CEDEFOP) (2011). Learning while working. Success stories of workplace learning in nine countries. www.cedefop.org.

Evans, K. and Rainbird, H. (2002). The significance of workplace learning for a 'learning society'. In K. Evans, P. Hodkinson, L. Unwin (eds.), *Working to Learn: Transforming Learning in the Workplace* (7–28). London: Routledge.

Findlay, A. M., Li, F. L. N., Jowett, A. J., and Skeldon, R. (1996). Skilled international migration and the global city: a study of expatriates in Hong Kong. *Transactions of the Institute of British Geographers*, 49–61.

Fozdar, F. and Torezani, S. (2008). Discrimination and well-being: Perceptions of refugees in Western Australia. *International Migration Review*, 42(1), 30–63.

Frankfurt, H. G. (1971). Freedom of the Will and the Concept of a Person. *Journal of Philosophy*, 68(1), 5–20.

Frankfurt, H G. (1988). Freedom of the will and the concept of a person. In M. F. Goodman (ed.), *What is a Person?* (127–144). Clifton, NJ: Humana Press.

Gallagher, E. N. and Vella-Brodrick, D. A. (2008). Social support and emotional intelligence as predictors of subjective well-being. *Personality and Individual Differences*, 44(7), 1551–1561.

Gerhards, J. and Hans, S. (2013). Transnational human capital, education, and social inequality. Analyses of international student exchange. *Zeitschrift für Soziologie*, 42(2), 99–117.

Grabowska-Lusińska, I. and Okólski, M. (2009). *Emigracja ostatnia?* Warszawa: Wydawnictwo Naukowe Scholar.

Grabowska, I. and Jastrzebowska, A. (2019). The impact of migration on human capacities of two generations of Poles: The interplay of the individual and the social in human capital approaches. *Journal of Ethnic and Migration Studies*, 47 (8), 1829–1847.

Grabowska, I. (2018). Social skills, workplaces and social remittances: A case of post-accession migrants. *Work, Employment and Society*, 32(5), 868–886.

Grabowska, I. (2019). *Otwierając głowy*. Warszawa: Wydawnictwo Naukowe Scholar.

Hagan, J. C., Hernández-León, R., Domonsant, J. C. (2015). *Skills of the "Unskilled". Work and Mobility among Mexican Migrants*. Oakland: University of California Press.

Hagan, J., Demonsant, J. L., and Chávez, S. (2014). Identifying and measuring the lifelong human capital of "Unskilled" migrants in the Mexico-US migratory circuit. *Journal on Migration and Human Security*, 2(2), 76–100.

Hagan, J. M., Wassink, J. (2016). New skills, new jobs: Return migration, skill transfers, and business formation in Mexico. *Social Problems*, 63(4): 513–533. https://doi.org/10.1093/socpro/spw02.

Harris, J. R. and Todaro, M. P. (1970). Migration, unemployment and development: A two-sector analysis. *The American Economic Review*, 60(1), 126–142.

Hendriks, M. and Bartram. D. (2019). Bringing happiness into the study of migration and its consequences: what, why, and how? *Journal of Immigrant and Refugee Studies*, 17(3), 279–298.

Heckman, J. J. (2000). Causal parameters and policy analysis in economics: A twentieth century retrospective. *The Quarterly Journal of Economics*, 115(1), 45–97.

Hobfoll, S. (1989). Conservation of Resources. A New Attempt at Conceptualizing Stress. *The American Psychologist*, 44(3): 513–524. doi:10.1037/0003-066X.44.3.513.

Hobfoll, S. (2001). The Influence of Culture, Community, and the Nested-Self in the Stress Process: Advancing Conservation of Resources Theory. *Applied Psychology: An International Review*, 50(3), 337–421.

Ilahi, N. (1999). Return migration and occupational change. Review of Development. *Economics*, 3(2), 170–186.

Janta, H. Jephcote, C., Williams, A., and Li, G. (2019). Returned migrants' acquisition of competencies: The contingencies of space and time. *Journal of Ethnic and Migration Studies*, 47(8), 1725–1739. doi:10.1080/1369183X.2019.1679408.

Jasinskaja-Lahti, I., Liebkind, K., Jaakkola, M., and Reuter, A. (2006). Perceived discrimination, social support networks, and psychological well-being among three immigrant groups. *Journal of Cross-Cultural Psychology*, 37(3), 293–311.

Jastrzebowska, A. (2020). *Dopasowanie kompetencyjne człowieka do pracy* [Person-job competence fit]. Warszawa: Wydawnictwo Scholar.

Khattab, N. and Fox, J. (2016). East-European immigrants responding to the recession in Britain: is there a trade-off between unemployment and over-qualification? *Journal of Ethnic and Migration Studies*, 42(11), 1774–1789.

Kwon, D. B. (2009). Human capital and its measurement. In The 3rd OECD World Forum on Statistics, Knowledge and Policy, Charting Progress, Building Visions, Improving Life, 27–30.

Li, F. L. N., Findlay, A. M., Jowett, A. J., and Skeldon, R. (1996). Migrating to learn and learning to migrate: a study of the experiences and intentions of international student migrants. *International Journal of Population Geography*, 2(1), 51–67.

Li, M., & Bray, M. (2006). Social class and cross-border higher education: Mainland Chinese students in Hong Kong and Macau. *Journal of International Migration and Integration*, 7(4), 407–424.

Lulle, A., Moroşanu, L., and King, R. (2018). And then came Brexit: Experiences and future plans of young EU migrants in the London region. *Population, Space and Place*, 24(1), e2122.

Lulle, A., Janta, H., and Emilsson, H. (2019). Introduction to the Special Issue: European youth migration: human capital outcomes, skills and competences. *Journal of Ethnic and Migration Studies*, 47(8), 1725–1739.

Luthans, F., Avey, J. B., Avolio, B. J., Norman, S., and Combs, G. (2006). Psychological capital development: Toward a micro intervention. *Journal of Organizational Behavior*, 27, 387–393.

Luthans, F. and Youssef, C. M. (2004). Human, social, and now positive psychological capital management. *Organizational Dynamics*, 33, 143–160.

Luthans, F. (2012). Psychological capital: Implications for HRD, retrospective analysis, and future directions and *Human Resource Development Quarterly*, 23, 1–8.

Luthans, F., Avey, J. B. Clapp-Smith, R., and Li, W. (2008). More evidence on the value of Chinese workers' psychological capital: A potentially unlimited competitive resource? *International Journal of Human Resource Management*, 19, 818–827.

Luthans, F., Norman, S. M., Avolio, B. J., and Avey, J. B. (2008). The mediating role of psychological capital in the supportive organizational climate–employee performance relationship and *Journal of Organizational Behavior*, 29, 219–238.

Luthans, F., Vogelgesang, G. R., and Lester, P. B. (2006). Developing the psychological capital of resiliency. *Human Resource Development Review*, 5, 25–44.

Ma, Z. (2002). Social-capital mobilization and income returns to entrepreneurship: The case of return migration in rural China and *Environment and Planning A: Economy and Space Environment and Planning A*, 34(10), 1763–1784.

Massey, D.S. and Espinosa, K.E. (1997). What's driving Mexico-U.S. migration? A theoretical, empirical, and policy analysis. *American Journal of Sociology*, 102(4): 939–999.

Masten, A. S. and Reed, M. G. J. (2002). Resilience in development. In C. R. Snyder, and S. Lopez (eds.), *Handbook of Positive Psychology* (74–88). Oxford, UK: Oxford University Press.

McCormick, B. and Wahba, J. (2003). Return international migration and geographical inequality: The case of Egypt and *Journal of African Economies*, 12 (4), 500–532.

McGarry, O., Krisjane, Z., Sechi, G., MacÉinrí, P., Berzins, M., Apsite-Berina, E. (2019). Human capital and life satisfaction among circular migrants: an analysis of extended mobility in Europe. *Journal of Ethnic and Migration Studies*, 1–19.

Mincer, J. (1958). Investment in human capital and personal income distribution. *Journal of Political Economy*, 66(4), 281–302.

Mincer, J. (1974). Progress in Human Capital Analysis of the distribution of earnings (No. w0053). National Bureau of Economic Research.

Mountford, A. (1997). Can a brain drain be good for growth in the source economy? *Journal of Development Economics*, 53(2), 287–303.

National Research Council (2013). *Education for Life and Work: Developing Transferable Knowledge and Skills in the 21st Century, Committee on Defining Deeper Learning and 21st Century Skills*. Washington, DC: The National Academy Press.

Newman, A., Ucbasaran, D., Zhu, F. E. I., & Hirst, G. (2014). Psychological capital: A review and synthesis. *Journal of organizational behaviour*, 35(S1), S120–S138.

Nussbaum, M. C. (2011). *Creating Capabilities. The Human Development Approach*. Cambridge, MA: The Belknap/Harvard University Press.

OECD (2005). *The Definition and Selection of Key Competencies*. Paris: OECD. https://www.oecd.org/pisa/35070367.pdf.

Palovic, Z., Janta, H., and Williams, A. M. (2019). In search of global skill sets: manager perceptions of the value of returned migrants and the relational nature of knowledge. *Journal of Ethnic and Migration Studies*, 47(8), 1–18.

Polanyi, M. (1958). *Personal Knowledge: Towards a Post-Critical Philosophy*. London: Routledge and Kegan Paul.

Polanyi, M. (1966). *The Tacit Dimension*. London: Routledge and Kegan Paul.

Ramirez, H. and Hondagneu-Sotelo, P. (2009). Mexican immigrant gardeners: entrepreneurs or exploited workers? *Social Problems*, 56(1), 70–88.

Randell, H. (2016). Structure and agency in development-induced forced migration: The case of Brazil's Belo Monte Dam. *Population and environment*, 37(3), 265–287.

Reich, A. Z. (1992). How well do you pitch? Improving your classroom delivery skills. *Hospitality & Tourism Educator*, 4(3), 67–68.

Robertson, S., Harris, A., and Baldassar, L. (2018). Mobile transitions: A conceptual framework for researching a generation on the move. *Journal of Youth Studies*, 21(2), 203–217.

Robinson, V. and Carey, M. (2000). Peopling skilled international migration: Indian doctors in the UK. *International Migration*, 38(1), 89–108.

Scheier, M. F., Carver, C. S., and Bridges, M. W. (2001). Optimism, pessimism, and psychological well-being. In E. C. Chang (ed.), *Optimism and pessimism: Implications for theory, research, and practice* (198–216). Washington DC: APA.

Schultz, T. W. (1961). Investment in human capital. *The American economic review*, 51(1), 1–17.

Seligman, M. E. P. (1998). *Learned optimism*. New York, NY: Pocket Books.

Sen, A. (2000). *Development as Freedom*. New York: Anchor Books.

Sen, A. (1997). Human capital and human capability. *World Development*, 25(12), 1959–1961.

Sen, A. (1979). Interpersonal comparisons of welfare. In *Economics and human welfare* (183–201). Cambridge: Academic Press.

Siedlecki, K. L., Salthouse, T. A., Oishi, S., and Jeswani, S. (2014). The relationship between social support and subjective well-being across age. *Social indicators research*, 117(2), 561–576.

Sjaastad, L. A. (1962). The costs and returns of human migration. *Journal of Political Economy*, 70(5, 2), 80–93.

Smith, C. (2011). *What is a Person? Rethinking Humanity, Social Life, and the Moral Good from the Person up*. Chicago: University of Chicago Press.

Snyder, C. R., Sympson, S., Ybasco, F., Borders, T., Babyak, M., and Higgins, R. (1996). Development and validation of the state hope scale. *Journal of Personality and Social Psychology*, 70, 321–335.

Stajkovic, A. D. and Luthans, F. (1998). Self-efficacy and work-related performance: A meta- analysis. *Psychological Bulletin*, 124, 240–261.

Staniscia, B., Deravignone, L., González-Martín, B., and Pumares, P. (2019). Youth mobility and the development of human capital: is there a Southern European model? *Journal of Ethnic and Migration Studies*, 47(8), 1866–1882.

Tomescu-Dubrow, I. (2015). International Experience and labour market success: Analysing panel data from Poland. *Polish Sociological Review*, 3(191), 259–276.

Tugade, M. M. and Fredrickson, B. L. (2004). Resilient individuals use positive emotions to bounce back from negative emotional experiences. *Journal of Personality and Social Psychology*, 86, 320–333.

Wassink, J. (2020). International migration experience and entrepreneurship: Evidence from Mexico. *World Development*, 136, 105077.

Williams, A. M., Baláž, V., and Wallace, C. (2004). International labour mobility and uneven regional development in Europe: Human capital, knowledge and entrepreneurship. *European Urban and Regional Studies*, 11(1), 27–46.

Williams, A. M., Baláž, V. (2005). What human capital, which migrants? Returned skilled migration to Slovakia from the UK. *International Migration Review*, 39 (2), 439–468.

Williams, A. M. and Baláž, V. (2008a). *International migration and knowledge*. Oxfordshire: Routledge.

Williams, A. M. and Baláž, V. (2008b). International return mobility, learning and knowledge transfer: A case study of Slovak doctors. *Social Science and Medicine*, 67(11), 1924–1933.

World Economic Forum (2017). Insight Report. The Global Human Capital Report 2017. Preparing People for the Future of Work. Cologny: World Economic Forum.

Young, M. Y. (2001). Moderators of stress in Salvadoran refugees: The role of social and personal resources. *International Migration Review*, 35(3): 840–869.

3 Methodology and data sources

Introduction

This chapter aims to explain the methodological sources and the analytical references for the entire book. Its aims are, firstly, to explain the selection of data sources that are used to present arguments regarding migration effects related to informal human capital; and secondly, to propose a theoretically grounded analytical model, which considers the acquisition, transfer and application of informal human capital as a result of migration and visualizes the rationale for the structure of this book.

Some of us view the social world through numbers, others through human stories (Putnam, 2015). In this book we will attempt to include both perspectives. To begin with, we will outline our multi-level approach to the impacts of international migration on informal human capital (MigCap) by presenting: (1) the big, macro picture, using statistical data; (2) the middle, meso picture, using cross-case qualitative studies (with large numbers of participants); and (3) the small, micro picture using the stories of selected individuals.

In order to present this multi-picture analysis of migration and informal human capital, a multi-method and multi-source approach is required. We will therefore use desk research as well as secondary and primary data analysis from several research projects that we had the privilege of conducting.

This book contains robust quantitative evidence and numerous qualitative findings, as well as in-depth stories of migrants from two parts of the world – Central Europe and Mexico. While quantitative data can, to a limited extent, provide information about how migration impacts on informal human capital, it cannot show us how it was moulded in everyday life.

The big picture – the helicopter or bird-eye view, or the macro perspective – relates to the statistical picture of the impact of migration experience on human capital, with a special focus on informal resources.

DOI: 10.4324/9781003011545-3

The middle picture or meso perspective relates to localities, comprising local contexts and cross-case analyses of numerous qualitative data from various countries.

The small picture or micro perspective consists of close-up accounts of the migratory experiences of various individuals over the course of their lives.

This multi-picture approach to the impact of international migration on informal human capital will use various sources of migration data.

The challenges in obtaining migration data

It is difficult or even impossible to obtain representative migration data from both sending and receiving populations, for several reasons.

First of all, the freedom to move and take up employment in the countries of the European Economic Area (EEA), including the EU, makes it difficult to register flows and migration stocks through both official statistics and less official sources. Even in those destination countries that do have data on migrants, this data does not cover all ethnic groups, which makes it impossible to obtain complete data on a country's population residing outside its borders. Furthermore, modern migrants engage in circular movements and return mobility (King, 2017), implementing subsequent trips. This argument is particularly relevant for Central Europeans.

Secondly, even if finding migrants is theoretically possible using official statistics, e.g in the censuses of sending and receiving countries, which usually take place every ten years, many migrants avoid being registered in such censuses. This is especially the case if migrants worked informally in their migration careers. Migrants may also fail to be registered during censuses due to circular mobility.

Thirdly, it is always possible to carry out surveys targeted at migrants as well as the general population in which migrants may appear occasionally. However, none of these two instances makes it possible to acquire a random sample of migrants because there is no sampling frame for the migrant population.

Fourthly, the broader socio-demographic characteristics of migrants may – albeit very rarely, taking into account the soft skills of migrants – appear in other social surveys carried out outside public statistics. However, data from such surveys are subject to numerous analytical constraints, e.g. difficulties in distinguishing the sub-population of migrants within the survey, as they are usually not sub-sampled in any specific framework. The most frequently asked questions about migration concern the fact of staying or working abroad, the choice of destination country, and sometimes the date of departure, the duration of migration and, more rarely, the purpose of the stay.

Fifthly, qualitative data is much easier to obtain because the selection of migrants for a study is always purposeful and oriented towards specific characteristics associated with the purpose of the study, although this is still not without challenges. In recent years, the biggest challenge in qualitative research on migrants is the high saturation of social studies in the field of migration, as a result of which respondents can be reluctant to participate in them. Qualitative data can provide unique in-depth information about migrants, their activities, experiences, behaviours and attitudes, but will not show the impact of migration on any variable across the entire population. Qualitative data can also provide inspiration for in-depth analyses of available quantitative data sets. In mixed-method approaches, they can complement and deepen knowledge about migrants, processes, impacts and migration outcomes.

Data sources and collection

The table below indicates the countries covered in this book, and the titles of the relevant research projects, authors, methods and samplings, as well as the way we approached the data for the purpose of this book. We take into account countries where research concerning the informal components of human capital has been conducted: in Central Europe - Slovakia, Poland, Lithuania and in Mexico.

Indicators of informal human capital

In 2016, the European Commission proposed the *New Skill Agenda for Europe*, and in 2018, the *Key Competences for Lifelong Learning*, which both stated that having competences in general leads to employability and success. The documents emphasized the importance of competency gaps and mismatches in the modern labour market, where many people do not work according to their talents, while 40 percent of European employers have problems finding the right employees (cf. Jastrzebowska, 2020).

The acquisition, development and formation of skills is crucial for the labour market and should be carried out throughout life. Humans should have a rich set of competences, including social and transferable competences, to fulfil their potential in the modern world. Key transferable soft skills include the ability to work in a team, creative thinking, taking initiative and problem-solving. The documents also talk about meta-competences: building resilience and the ability to learn. The European Commission also mentions transversal skills, which enable the interpenetration of formal, hard and soft competences.

The 2018 document cited above defined eight key competences for lifelong learning: communication in the mother tongue; communication in

Table 3.1 Data sources by country

Country	Title of the study and methodology used to collect data	Samples		Literature sources	Approach to a source in this book
Poland (Central Europe)	1 BKL Representative survey: Human Capital in Poland 2010–2014	1	70000 non-migrants; 4000 migrants	Grabowska and Jastrzebowska (2019); Grabowska (2019); Grabowska and Jastrzebowska (under review)	Secondary and primary source Own analyses and own research Own projects; data re-analyses; primary data
	2 CAREERS Post-accession careers of Poles – biographical interviews (Grant No. 85021 Ministry of Science)	2	18 biographical interviews		
	3 HARMONIA Diffusion of Culture Through Social Remittances between Poland and The United Kingdom (Grant No. 179068 National Science Center Poland)	3	121 in-depth interviews		
	4 SONATA BIS Peer-groups and migration (Grant No. 300091 National Science Center Poland)	4	n=520 return Poles from the UK; comparable no. of Lithuanians and 34 IDIs with returnees.		
	5 DAINA CEEYouth online survey (Grant No. 393464 National Science Center Poland and Research Council of Lithuania)				

Country	Title of the study and methodology used to collect data	Samples	Literature sources	Approach to a source in this book
Slovakia (Central Europe)	1 Survey with semi-structured interviews with various occupational categories/subsamples of professional/managerial, student and au pair migrants who spent at least three months in the UK 2 Survey with Slovak migrants and returnees as a part of YMobility research project	1 186 semi-structured interviews with return migrants to the UK: (1) managers=64; (2) students=55; (3) au pairs=67 2 n=366	Williams and Baláž (2005)* Baláž at al., (2019)	Desk research
Lithuania (Central Europe)	CEEYouth online survey (Grant No. 393464 National Science Center Poland and Research Council of Lithuania)	n=216 of return Lithuanians from the UK; comparable with 500 Poles n=5 IDIs with returnees		Primary source; own research
Mexico	Survey In-depth interviews	n of return migrants to Leon N=200; M=172; F=28	Hagan, et al., (2014); Hagan, et al., (2015); Hagan, et al., (2019); Hagan and Wassink (2016, 2020)	Desk research

Country	Title of the study and methodology used to collect data	Samples	Literature sources	Approach to a source in this book
OECD data relating to all countries included in the analysis	"A profile of Immigrant Populations in the 21st Century. Data from OECD Countries"	National samples	OECD (2008)	Desk research

* The study of returned Slovak migrants is based on three subsamples of professional/managerial, student and au pair migrants, reflecting some of the diversity that characterizes skilled migration flows.

Source: own selection.

foreign languages; mathematical competences and basic scientific and technological competences; digital competences; learning to learn; social and civic competences; taking initiatives and entrepreneurship; and cultural awareness and expression.

Skills should be considered dynamically on three levels: (1) knowledge, i.e. facts, concepts, and ideas; (2) abilities to carry out activities, using knowledge to achieve results; and (3) attitudes, i.e. dispositions and state of mind to act and react to people, ideas and situations (European Commission, 2016). All three levels overlap and interpenetrate.

In 2005, the OECD published *The Definition and Selection of Key Competencies*, in which special attention was paid to three categories of competences (after: Rychen et al., 2003; Green, 2011): (1) interactive use of communication instruments (language, technology, etc.); (2) interactions in diverse social groups; and (3) autonomous operation. Reflexivity is at the centre of these competency categories.

The importance of intercultural competences in the contemporary global world is discussed by UNESCO (2013). UNESCO pays special attention to communication competences – language, dialogue, and non-verbal communication – and cultural competencies relating to identity, values, attitudes and beliefs. UNESCO emphasizes the ability of a person to move between cultures (cultural shifting) in relation to language, behaviour and gestures, reflexivity – i.e. the ability of a person to go beyond the sphere of their own experience in order to reflexively look at the world, consider what is happening, what it means and how to react to it – and agility, i.e. the ability of people to adapt to changes in the world. UNESCO points out that none of the abovementioned competences works alone in the social world; intercultural competences work in bundles.

In this book, the cognitive, mind dimension consists of sub-dimensions: the ability to quickly summarise large amounts of text, logical thinking, analysis of facts and the constant learning of new things.

The intrapersonal, soft dimension includes the following sub-dimensions: independent decision-making, entrepreneurship and showing initiative, creativity – being innovative, coming up with new solutions – resistance to stress and timely implementation of planned activities.

The interpersonal, soft dimension includes the following sub-dimensions: cooperation in groups, easy networking with colleagues or clients, being communicative and communicating clearly and resolving conflicts between people.

The manual, maker dimension covers sub-dimensions of non-validated and non-certified technical skills relating to the operation of machines and hardware; craft skills; all hands-on skills; e.g. carpentry, all kinds of painting (in the broadest sense: walls, murals, paintings and canvas, restoration, making professional makeup, nails, flowery, interior decorations, etc.). The manual dimension also considers dexterity, i.e. the ability to use one's hands in a skilful, coordinated way to grasp and manipulate objects.

The dimension of life skills relating to wellbeing includes sub-dimensions concerned with life and job satisfactions in relation to both mental and physical state of health. It is also connected to the feeling of "normal life" or "good life" as a result of migration (Galasinska and Kozlowska, 2009).

In order to measure each component of MigCap we feed these indicators with both quantitative and qualitative data from various research projects and desk research analyses. For Slovakia and Mexico, we were limited to information available through desk research; for Poland and Lithuania, there are more options enabling a wider spectrum of analyses, as most of the data used is derived from research projects that we personally oversaw (see Table 3.2).

The data regarding the indicators of MigCap is mostly based on self-reports and self-assessments; but there are also some cases in our data where we asked the others – migrants' followers, recipients of potential transfer (e.g. HARMONIA research project).

Analytical model and summary

This methodological chapter also presents the analytical model of this monograph. The model (Figure 3.1) is derived from the introduction and theoretical discussion, which explored the theoretical clues of migration-

Table 3.2 Components of informal human capital and their indicators

Components of Informal Human Capital (MigCap)	Indicators
MIND SKILLS	Cognitive skills – working knowledge learned informally through observing, communicating and doing; capacity to learn
SOFT SKILLS	Personal/people skills – internal (reflexivity) and social, interpersonal
MAKER SKILLS	Manual, technical – non-validated, non-certified; acquired and practiced on the spot
LIFE SKILLS	Life satisfaction and job satisfaction in seeking a normal, good life, linked to well-being.

Source: Author's elaboration.

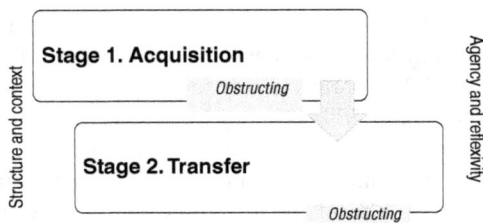

Figure 3.1 Analytical model
Source: Author's elaboration based on Grabowska (2019).

impacted informal human capital. The model does not directly relate to the nature of MigCap, but to the process of its acquisition, development, enhancement, transfer and application. The model also covers the process of obstructing the acquisition and transfer of informal human capital. The processes of acquiring and transferring MigCap take place in structural contexts, and at each stage includes the agency and reflexivity of individuals.

In order for something to be transferred, it must first be acquired. Stage 1 of the analytical model relates to the acquisition of MigCap in migration processes and also applies to the processes of forming and developing and strengthening the already existing informal human capital. Stage 2 concerns the transfer of informal human capital between areas of human activity (work, organisations, home, hobbies), between sending and receiving places and between life stages. At the stages of acquisition and transfer, the acquisition of informal human capital may be obstructed or resisted. Both stages are related to the structural conditions in which they occurred. Agency and the different types of reflexivity of migrants are taken into account.

In order to explain the selection of countries studied in this book, the following chapter presents the socio-demographic profiles of migrants from Central Europe – Poland, Slovakia, Lithuania and migrants from Mexico. Chapter 5 of this book is devoted to the first stage of the analytical model and discusses the acquisition, development and enhancement of MigCap. Chapter 6 concerns the second stage indicated in the analytical model above, and discusses the transfer and various applications of informal human capital after return.

References

Baláž, V., Williams, A. M., Moravčíková, K., and Chrančoková, M. (2019). What competences, which migrants? Tacit and explicit knowledge acquired via migration. *Journal of Ethnic and Migration Studies*, 47 (8), 1758–1774.

European Commission (2016). A new skills agenda for Europe. Communication from the Commission to the European Parliament, The Council, The European Economic and Social Committee and The Committee of the Regions, European Commission, Brussels.

Galasińska, A. and Kozlowska, O. (2009). *"Either" and "Both" – the changing concept of living space among Polish post-communist migrants to the United Kingdom. Globalization and language in contact: Scale, migration and communicative practices.* New York: Continuum.

Grabowska, I. (2019). *Otwierajac glowy. Migracje i kompetencje spoleczne.* Warsaw: Scholar.

Grabowska, I. and Jastrzebowska, A. (2019). The impact of migration on human capacities of two generations of Poles: The interplay of the individual and the social in human capital approaches. *Journal of Ethnic and Migration Studies*, 47 (8), 1829–1847.

Grabowska, I. and Jastrzebowska, A. (under review). *Migrant Informal Human Capital of Returnees.*

Green, J. (2011). What is Skill? An Inter-Disciplinary Synthesis. LLAKES Research Paper 20. London: Centre for Learning and Life Chances in Knowledge Economies and Societies. http://citeseerx.ist.psu.edu/viewdoc/download; jsessionid=7A3FF633369DF7738E9CD56606835329?doi=10 1.1.673.2343a ndrep=rep1andtype=pdf.

Hagan, J. C., Hernández-León, R., and Domonsant, J. C. (2015). *Skills of the "Unskilled". Work and Mobility among Mexican Migrants.* Oakland: University of California Press.

Hagan, J., Demonsant, J. L., and Chávez, S. (2014). Identifying and measuring the lifelong human capital of "Unskilled" migrants in the Mexico-US migratory circuit. *Journal on Migration and Human Security*, 2(2), 76–100.

Hagan, J. M. and Wassink, J. (2016). New skills, new jobs: Return migration, skill transfers, and business formation in Mexico. *Social Problems*, 63(4): 513–533. doi:10.1093/socpro/spw021.

Hagan, J. M. and Wassink, J. T. (2020). Return migration around the world: An integrated agenda for future research, *Annual Review of Sociology*, 46, 533–552.

Hagan, J. M., Wassink, J. T. , and Castro, B. (2019). A longitudinal analysis of resource mobilization among forced and voluntary return migrants in Mexico. *Journal of Ethnic and Migration Studies*, 45(1), 170–189.

Jastrzebowska, A. (2020). *Dopasowanie kompetencyjne czlowieka do pracy* [Person-job competence fit]. Warszawa: Wydawnictwo Scholar.

King, R. (2017). Theorising new European youth mobilities. *Population, Space and Place*, https://doi.org/10.1002/psp.2117.

Organisation for Economic Co-operation and Development (2008). *A profile of immigrant populations in the 21st century: data from OECD countries.* Paris: OECD Publishing.

Putnam, R. D. (2015). *Our kids. The American Dream in Crisis.* New York: Simon and Schuster.

Rychen, D. S., Salganik, L. H., and McLaughlin, M. E. (eds.) (2003). *Key competencies for a successful life and well-functioning society*. Göttingen: Hogrefe Publishing.

UNESCO (2013). *Intercultural Competences. Conceptual and Operational Framework*. Paris: UNESCO.

Williams, A. M. and Baláž, V. (2005). What human capital, which migrants? Returned skilled migration to Slovakia from the UK, *International Migration Review*, 39(2), 439–468.

4 Profiles of migrating and returning Mexicans and Central Europeans

Introduction

This chapter aims to profile Mexican migrants crossing the border between Mexico and the USA, one of the most protected borders in the world and Central European (CE) migrants, also called movers, who are mobile within the space of the European Union (EU) freedom of movement.[1] We intend to profile migrants on two migration axes for the following arguments. Firstly, CE movers, who can migrate freely between countries in the EU and European Economic Area (EEA), without borders and with no restrictions in accessing EU labour markets, and Mexicans, for whom both crossing the border and entering the labour market are subject to innumerable restrictions and constraints. Secondly, CE movers are one of the highest-educated migrant groups among OECD countries,[2] while Mexicans rank among the lowest-educated.

This chapter is based on two sources of data: (1) usable to make comparisons from the OECD datasets (2008), which among others enables comparisons between migrants from the new EU countries and Mexican movers – presented in the second part of this chapter; and (2) non-usable to make comparisons of data sources specific for Mexicans and for Central Europeans, collected by various institutions and researchers using various methodologies. The analysis of this data seeks to profile socio-demographically international migrants from Mexico and Central Europe in order to demonstrate the formal dimensions of human capital.

In this book we argue – among other points – that in order to understand the acquisition and transfer of formal and informal human capital, it is important to look at the whole course of migration: emigration, immigration, return migration and re-migration, both under circumstances of free mobility – CE movers – and under circumstances of restricted migration – Mexican migrants. Although there was a time in history when the migration of Central Europeans to Western Europe and the USA was

DOI: 10.4324/9781003011545-4

subject to many restrictions, while Mexicans were once able to move back and forth between the USA and Mexico much more freely than in the 21st century – in fact, this relative non-restriction on Mexican migration lasted until the late 1970s, perhaps even longer. For Central Europe, this situation changed in 1989/1990, when travelling restrictions were lifted following the breakdown of communism – although the free movement of workers was only extended to include CE migrants when the relevant countries became members of the EU in May 2004. The inverse developments affecting Mexican migrants occurred in the early years of the 1980s, when the American administration introduced restrictions for circulatory moves, meaning that migrants who had left their families in Mexico were required to either bring their families for long-term settlement in the USA, or return to Mexico.

Profiles of migrating and returning Mexicans

> Throughout the latter half of the twentieth century, Mexican migration to the United States grew steadily, establishing itself as the largest binational labour flow in the world.
>
> (Abel and Sander, 2014; cf. Wassink, 2020: 10).

The Mexican census of 2000 was designed to gather information about the international migration experience of Mexicans[3]. The questionnaire asked families to indicate whether they had any family members who had emigrated abroad during the period of the last five years. Those who did were asked a series of questions about the migrants' sex, age at the time of last emigration, country of migration, and place of living during census. The findings showed that 97 percent of the people reported migration to the USA between 1995 and 2000. The second destination country was Canada, which was disproportionate to the US migration and amounted to 1 percent. The census also revealed a number of returnees to Mexico and their following migration during census time. The percentage of Mexican migrants who were covered by the census in the US in 2000 was nearly 76 percent, while nearly 17 percent returned to Mexico (Caponi, 2006: 6).

Clearly the USA is the leading destination country for migrating Mexicans. Annual immigration flows peaked in 2000, when 700 000 Mexicans migrated to the USA. The number of Mexican-born immigrants living in the USA reached the all-time high number of 12.5 million in 2007. Their influx had been very dynamic: 760 000 lived in the USA in 1970 (Hazán, 2017). In the 1980s and 1990s, migration became more settlement-oriented as a result of more restrictive US border controls and migration policy. This also led to more definitive return migration, especially among migrants who had left their families behind in Mexico (Hazán, 2017).

Massey and Espinosa determined that one of the fundamental forces pushing Mexicans to the USA is human capital formation which is a crucial argument for this book. By researching 25 Mexican communities, they discovered that the most important component of human capital is "migration experience, crossing the border, living in the United States, working in the U.S. labour market, and negotiating U.S. housing markets" (Massey and Espinosa, 1997: 989), which in fact can be classified as some components of informal human capital – the subject matter of this book. They proved that the more experience in the USA a migrant has, the more he/she will migrate, both as a documented and as an undocumented migrant. Massey and Espinoza (1997) also showed that while reinforcing human capital, Mexican migrants also accumulate social capital. This means that the more migratory experience a migrant has, the more friends and relatives of that person will decide to migrate as well. National surveys show that every third Mexican migrated to the United States at some stage of their life course (Camp, 1993). Massey and Espinosa (1997) conclude that after 50 years of ongoing movements, migratory-impacted human capital is also widely diffused in Mexico.

As a result of the global financial crisis of 2007–2009, changing demographic and economic characteristics in Mexico, and increased policy and border restrictions by the US administration, annual migration from Mexico to the United States fell 70 percent between 2000 and 2010 (Hanson, 2009; Passel et al., 2012; Villarreal, 2014). The same factors increased voluntary and forced return migration to Mexico. Between 2005 and 2014, 2.4 million Mexican immigrants returned home from the United States, twice as much as the number of returnees during the preceding decade (Gonzalez-Barrera, 2015; Wassink, 2020: 10).

Mexicans were the immigrant group most affected by the economic downturn of 2007. Figures from the Pew Centre[4] show that in the first quarter of 2007, the number of unemployed Mexican immigrants in the US was 391,000. By the first quarter of 2008, this figure had grown by another 233,000 humans – an increase of nearly 60 percent in one year, with the majority of jobs lost in construction.

Analysis of data from the US and Mexican censuses reveals, among others, that it is the lowest-educated and the highest-educated Mexicans who gain the most from migrating to the US. Middle-educated Mexicans – generally having six or nine years of schooling – have relatively lower gains and therefore are less likely to migrate (Caponi, 2006: 29–30).

We know however from censuses that from 2005 and 2010 there were 1.08 million returnees to Mexico predominantly from the US and other destinations. Nearly 70 percent of returnees were male and nearly 30 percent were female, with an increasing return flow of women (Hazán, 2017: 18). (…) The

ENOE[5] also shows that most of these returnees had low educational levels: the majority – close to 70 percent – had only elementary and middle school education. However, from 2008, in the wake of the economic crisis, the proportion of return migrants with high school and university degrees increased by a few percentage points.[6]

Since 2007 Mexicans have been returning to their home country *en masse*, to the point that the net migration from Mexico to the USA was zero – a phenomenon that had never taken place since the 1930s, when Mexicans were expelled and forced to leave as a result of the Great Depression. Between 2010 and 2015, nearly 1.4 million Mexicans returned from the USA to Mexico, the majority of whom had no intention to move again which is huge potential for the transfer of human capital.

There is also some evidence that instead of returning to their home cities, towns and villages, many post-2007 returnees have elected to seek opportunities elsewhere in Mexico instead (cf. Massferer and Roberts, 2012). Masferrer and Roberts (2012) showed how the socioeconomic characteristics of returning migrants in Mexico have been changing. They relate the growing diversification of the geography of return migration within Mexico.

Women, although not that visible in the literature of return migration, constitute a sizable portion of the return migration flow, a bit more than every third returnee to Mexico is a woman, and their potential economic contribution should not be overlooked (Parrado and Gutierrez, 2016).

Business formation also plays an important role in activities of returnees to Mexico, for example Massey and Parrado, 1998; Wassink, 2020). Massey and Parrado (1998) discuss various domains of entrepreneurship activity after returning to Mexico. In order to understand business formation after return they consider various aspects of opportunity structures: (1) personal resources such as Mexican labour force experience; years of schooling; occupation skills; US migrant experience; being a migrant; USA papers; (2) household resources such as property ownership; number of dependent children; land and home ownership; other businesses owned; economic remittances – *migradollars*; (3) community assets such as preparatory school; bank in the community; telephone and other services; (4) local market potential such as earnings; self-employed; females in manufacturing; rural economy; municipal population and economic remittances; (5) national macroeconomic conditions such as interest rates; devaluation; inflation rate; no. of businesses. They found that when studying business formation, one must take into account a wider context and a wider set of variables. Through a study of 30 Mexican communities, they revealed a positive picture and therefore positive relationship between migrant entrepreneurship and the economic remittances. Whether Mexicans choose to set up a business following return to their home country depends on personal and family resources and family economic situation. Household heads are more likely to set up businesses if they are young, well-educated and skilled and if they are married and come from property-owning households and educated families. They also set up their own business more frequently if they live in industrially developed communities with high wages, high levels of self-employment, rapid inflation and high interest rates. They also found a positive relation between economic remittances and the setting up of their own businesses – the more money they bring back the more they are prone to set up their own firm (Massey and Parrado, 1998).

Most recently Wassink (2020) brought together analyses of 170 Mexican communities in order to assess the possibility of becoming an entrepreneur and the role of migratory experience in doing business. The study showed that migration experience is positively correlated with entrepreneurship, especially by documented migrants. The longer a migrant's migration experience, the more human capital and economic remittances they can accumulate, which can subsequently be used for such purposes as setting up one's own business. It is also important to note that the population of self-employed returnees is not homogeneous – they vary in terms of duration of US migratory experience, educational level, volume of economic remittances, and destination of their new business and sector.

The analyses of three Mexican Censuses (1990, 2000 and 2010) proved that in 1990, both male and female returnees to Mexico were more likely to establish businesses and to be self-employed than after 2010, following the economic downturn (Parrado and Gutierrez, 2016). International migrants were always more likely to set up businesses than non-migrants and internal migrants, also after 2010 (Parrado and Gutierrez, 2016). Parrado and Gutierrez also highlighted that "return migrants are able to translate experience and knowledge acquired abroad into higher wages in the Mexican labour market" (Parrado and Gutierrez, 2016: 110).

Mexico is also a big sender of unauthorised migrants. Massey, Durand and Pren (2016) proved that any enforcement of border control intensifies the flow of undocumented migrants from Mexico.

Mexico also receives the largest number of migrants deported from the United States. The estimates offered by resources based on national statistical data present a very wide range: between 5 and 35 percent of returning migrants are deportees (ibid.).

To sum up, throughout the decades, the socio-demographic profiles of Mexican migrants did not change much compared to the profiles of returnees. In fact the biggest differences relate to returnees, especially when looking at three points of time of Mexican censuses in 1990, 2000 and 2010. The global financial crisis of 2008 changed the opportunities in the destination countries, especially in the USA, as well as in sending Mexico, which impacted on returning migrants. After the crisis, many returnees were inactive for some time (women more frequently than men), and set up fewer businesses than in the 1990s. There were also fewer opportunities for the transfer of knowledge and skills to local economies, as these also suffered from the crisis but still the transfer has been taking place.

Profiles of mobile (returning) Central Europeans

When looking at the history of Central and Eastern Europe through the prism of mobility, three periods should be distinguished. Firstly, the period between 1950, after mass displacements directly related to the effects of World War II, and 1989, with particular emphasis on the last two decades, i.e. the declining phase of communism, when, after the collapse of political and economic structures, previously unknown migration opportunities opened up. Secondly, the phase of systemic transition initiated in 1989 and thirdly, subsequent years, which brought drastic changes in all spheres of life of Central and Eastern European residents, including geographical mobility.

(Fihel et al., 2007: 176)

In the early 1990s, after the Iron Curtain had fallen, Central Europe began a complex post-communist political, economic and social transformation, known as a *system transformation*, which symbolically lasted until the countries of Central Europe acceded to the European Union (EU) in May 2004. The Central European countries under study in this book are Poland, Slovakia and Lithuania, each of which has been affected by communism in different ways. Poland was a so-called satellite country of the USSR. Slovakia was also a satellite country, but at the time it was part of the larger conglomerate of Czechoslovakia, which split into the Czech Republic and Slovak Republic in 1992. Lithuania, on the other hand, had been incorporated into the USSR, along with the other Baltic States, Latvia and Estonia. The independence of Poland was restored in 1989; Lithuania regained its independence in 1990, and Slovakia in 1993, after its separation from the Czech Republic. The societies and economies of these three countries have since undergone far-reaching reforms and deep social changes. Large post-communist factories and rural cooperatives were shut down, causing high levels of unemployment. In the 1990s, these changes also prompted outmigration flows, primarily to EU countries; many of these migratory movements were seasonal and either based on bilateral agreements or undocumented, on the basis of so-called "false tourism". Poland was the leader of outmigration among the three CE countries in that period, having the largest population[7]. One further aspect that these three CE countries had in common in the 1990s was seasonal migration to Germany. Until the EU enlargement in May 2004, Germany was the leading destination country for all three societies. The migratory flows from CE countries to Germany mostly concerned seasonal migration for periods of up to three months, based on bilateral agreements (see Table 4.1).

The biggest historical enlargement of the EU, when multiple countries from Central and Eastern Europe – including the three under study – joined the union,[8] had just justified some of these movements of the 1990s because the EU membership allowed for work and residency registration and longer, unlimited stays abroad. The dynamism of the migratory movements from Poland, Lithuania and, to a lesser extent, Slovakia, were growing rapidly as new age cohorts were joining the outflowing populations, including large numbers of recent university graduates who were unable to find work at home. Due to wage differences and currency exchange rates, usually four or five times higher abroad, it is attractive for many Central Europeans to take jobs abroad, even below and not matched with their formal qualifications (see Tables 4.2 and 4.3).

On 1 May 2004, Poles, Lithuanians and Slovakians became subject to the full free movement of persons and unrestricted rights to be employed in the UK, Ireland and Sweden. Other EU countries introduced various restrictions (see Table 4.4).

Table 4.1 Population of migrants in Germany from Lithuania, Poland and the Slovak Republic around 2000

CE country	Population in Germany
Lithuania	8 042
Poland	291 673
Slovakia	1 097

Source: Fihel et al. (2007: 59).

Table 4.2 Occupations of the foreign born population, share of the employed population aged 15+ [in per cent]

Country of birth	Professionals	Technicians	Operators
Poland	13.1	24.7	62.2
Slovak Republic	18.4	23.8	57.8

*Data for Lithuania is not included in these statistics of the 50 main origin countries in the OECD area.
Source: OECD (2008).

Table 4.3 Fields of study of the foreign born population, share of the employed population aged 15+ [in per cent]

Country of birth	Education and health	Humanities and social sciences	Science and engineering	Other
Poland	23.0	33.3	39.4	4.3
Slovak Republic	24.5	29.0	41.9	4.6

*Data for Lithuania is not included in these statistics of the 50 main origin countries in the OECD area.
Source: OECD (2008).

Table 4.4 EU enlargements transitional provisions

Level of restrictions	First Phase, 1 May 2004–30 April 2006	Second Phase, 1 May 2006–30 April 2009	First Phase for Bulgaria and Romania, 1 January 2007–31 December 2008
Open access to labour market	UK, Ireland and Sweden	Finland, Greece, Portugal, Luxembourg, Netherlands, Spain lifted restrictions during the second phase	Czech Republic, Cyprus, Estonia, Finland, Latvia, Lithuania, Poland, Slovenia, Slovakia, Sweden
Work permit system	Austria, Belgium, Denmark, Finland, France, Germany, Greece, Italy, Luxembourg, Netherlands, Portugal, Spain	Austria, Belgium, France, Denmark, Germany, Italy	Austria, Belgium, Denmark, Finland, France, Germany, Greece, Hungary, Ireland, Italy, Luxembourg, Malta, Netherlands, Portugal, Spain, UK
Reduced restrictions for some professions		Belgium, France, Denmark, Germany	
Additional restrictions for some professions			Austria, Germany

Source: European Commission; Pollard et al. (2008).

Soon after the enlargement of the EU in May 2004, the UK became the main destination country for all Central European countries discussed in this book (see Table 4.5 and Table 4.6).

The dynamically growing emigration lasted until the global financial crisis of 2008, which unevenly affected Poland, Slovakia and Lithuania. Of the CE countries, Lithuania was the most severely affected by the global financial crisis, which brought a paradox for Lithuanian migrants to migrate from a country in crisis, to countries in crisis. Nevertheless, migration continued. Following the financial crisis, return migration increased, although these flows consisted largely of the lower-educated and migrants whose contracts had ended, who returned to their localities of origin, usually rural areas. Higher-educated migrants and migrants from urban areas mostly remained abroad throughout the financial crisis.

Mobility from and return mobility to Central European countries continued after the crisis ended, until the occurrence of Brexit[9]. In the aftermath of the referendum that led to the UK's exit from the EU, researchers investigated the influences of Brexit on migrants. The impact of Brexit for all EU migrants should not be generalised and equalised (cf. Lulle, King, Dvorakova and Szkudlarek, 2018; cf. Klimaviciute et al., 2020: 130).

Table 4.5 Arrivals in the UK 2004–2005 (in thousands)

CE country	2004	2005
Lithuania	79	133
Poland	646	1127
Slovak Republic	106	189

Source: cf. Fihel et al (2007: 61).

Table 4.6 Polish and Lithuanian populations in the UK, various years

	Census 2001	LFS 2004 Q Rank among immigrants		LFS 2007Q4 Rank among immigrants	
Polish nationals	no data	53 000	13	447 000	1
Polish-born	58 000	84 000	14	458 000	2
Lithuanian nationals	no data	-	-	51 000	23
Lithuanians-born	4 200	-	-	52 000	32

Source: Pollard et al. (2008).

According to the Intra-EU Mobility Report 2020 (Fries-Tersch et al., 2020), Poland was among the top five sending countries of the EU. Around half of all EU movers, mostly from Central and Eastern Europe, reside in either Germany or the UK and one in four movers reside in Spain, Italy or France. The share of those who returned to their origins in the EU compared to those who left in 2017 increased to 72 percent (66 percent in 2016), meaning that for every four people who leave, three return. Return mobility[10] increased in 2017 in the EU, with around 723,000 nationals returning to their country of origin. Compared to the number of nationals who left their country in the same year, the ratio of return mobility in 2017 was 72 percent (cf. Fries-Tersch et al., 2020).

In 2018, EU movers primarily worked in the sectors of manufacturing, wholesale and retail trade, construction, and accommodation and food services. 36 percent of all active EU-28 movers were highly educated, 40 percent had medium education, and 23 percent had a lower education level. Every five EU mover was employed in low-skill or elementary occupations that require only a lower secondary education degree; another fifth were employed in high-skill occupations. It is worth remembering however that approximately 60 percent of all migrants were employed in occupations with medium skill level requirements. As regards the mobility periods, data from the European Labour Force Survey showed that of all movers who spent at least one year in a host country, called in the EU statistics - long-term movers - more than 50 percent did not remain abroad for longer than four years. Shorter migration periods from one to four years have become significantly more common since 2004. The EU-13 countries had the highest proportion of returnees, accounting for 86 percent of the inflow to Romania and 52 percent for Poland. Six other countries: Hungary, Bulgaria, Croatia, Lithuania, Estonia and Latvia had rates close to 50 percent. In Poland on four persons leaving, two return. Several other countries of origin had lower proportions of return mobility than Poland: Lithuania (24 percent), Latvia (33 percent), Slovenia (29 percent) and Slovakia (33 percent).

Return mobility to Lithuania was since the economic crisis in 2008 primarily dominated by movers of young working age. In 2009 and 2017, 60 percent of all returnees were between 20 and 39 years old. Around 30 percent of this group were of very young working age (20–29) in 2009, increasing to 40 percent in 2017. The age distribution of the outflows of both Poland and Lithuania was very similar to that of returnees in 2009 and 2017. In fact, the ratios of 20- to 29-year-olds were slightly higher in the outflows than among returnees. Migration from Lithuania is largely dominated by young and very young working-age movers, but around one third of these movers return to Lithuania after only a few years (Fries-Tersch et al., 2020).

Return migration to Lithuania has grown significantly since 2010, although it experienced a brief decline in 2016. According to the official statistics, an approximate total of 102 000 Lithuanian citizens registered their return between 2011 and 2016 – about 17,000 per year. The official data only reveals a partial picture because a significant share of migration from Lithuania is short-term or undeclared (Žvalionyte, 2014). With the data available in the dedicated surveys we can notice that the average Lithuanian returnee is relatively young (25–36 years old), has lived abroad for between two and four years and chose to return primarily because they wanted to reunite with their family and live in a familiar cultural environment. Roughly one third of returnees returned from the UK due to the fact that before Brexit the UK was the key destination country (Barcevičius and Žvalionyte, 2012; Barcevičius and Žvalionyte, 2015). Many young Lithuanian returnees studied abroad or increased their human capital through work experience (Barcevičius, 2016 – DAINA CEEYouth grant application; Lithuanian Team).

In 2009 return mobility to Poland was dominated by 20–29 year old young adults and they constituted 60 percent of return flow. Since then the age of returnees has increased. In 2017, the share of 20–29 years old young adults dropped to 10 percent, while that of 30–39 year olds increased to 30 percent. The outflows however consisted primarily of young Polish movers, the average age being less than 30 years (Kindler, 2018). The share of this age group below 30 also dropped among those leaving Poland between 2010 and 2017, which suggests that mobility in general became less prominent among young Polish citizens, compared to other age groups. It is linked with Poland's economic growth in the decade 2010–2020, which made youngsters spend more time in education and increased their opportunities on the labour market (Fries-Tersch et al., 2020).

Polish return migration peaked in 2007, when 200,000 migrants returned to Poland from various destinations (Anacka, 2010). However, the financial crisis did not cause massive return flows, but changed the geographies of the destination countries. The ratio of returnees from Great Britain was lower than the proportion of those Poles leaving for the UK (Anacka, 2010). Young adults aged 20–29 and university graduates were not eager to return. While survey data indicated that outmigration was driven by economic reasons, the return moves were primarily motivated by family reasons (Szymańska et al., 2012). Iglicka (2009) noted that about 40 percent of returnees with higher education were unable to find work in Poland, thus forcing this group to subsequent mobility.[11]

The time that returning migrants have spent abroad does appear to yield certain advantages in the areas of human capital and labour market performance. Several studies of return migration identified improvements in the income of migrants after return (Martin and Radu, 2012; Hazans, 2008)[. Findings concerning gender are mixed or not included in the study of income bonus (Iara 2008: 12) and the comparability of studies is questionable as the data used is often country-specific, and the types of analysis as well as the databases used vary per study. In Iara's (2008) study, young and male return migrants earned an average wage premium of 30 percent on CEE labour markets if they had Western European work experience. Interestingly, no wage bonus can be found for labour market experience in other CEE countries. As a possible explanation for the identified wage premium, Iara (2008) posited an increase in the skills of these migrants, and therefore their human capital, as a result of learning on the job in countries with higher technological development, which also added to knowledge diffusion in CEE countries (Lang and Nadler, 2014, RE-TURN research project).

Findings regarding the level of education of returnees vary with regard to the ability to enhance career opportunities or its fragmentation. Martin and Radu (2012) determined that returning migrants to Central Europe are more likely to be either not participating in the labour market or self-employed than dependently employed.

Migrating Central Europeans and Mexicans in a comparative OECD dataset: a profile of migrants in the 21st century

The comparative analysis of migrating Central Europeans and Mexicans presented in this subchapter is based on a single harmonised source of OECD data. It is derived from the dataset *A Profile of Immigrant Populations in the 21st Century. Data from OECD Countries*, which is unique in that it enables comparisons to be drawn between the profiles of migrating Mexicans and Central Europeans. Unfortunately, the amount of available information about the CE countries discussed in this book is limited; for this reason, most tables on the following pages do not include figures for Slovakia and Lithuania. In these cases, Poland must be taken as a representative for CE countries.

Looking at the general data (Table 4.7), it is noticeable that migration from the EU10 countries – the scope of which is somewhat wider than Central Europe, as it also includes Cyprus and Malta, although these are both very small countries – is less than half of Mexican migration (45 percent). Clear differences also emerge when profiling migrants from Mexico and Central Europeans.

Firstly, Mexican migration is masculinised, i.e. dominated by male migrants, while Central European migration is feminised: migrants are primarily female. This might have to do with the leading sectors of employment among migrants: Mexican migrants are primarily employed in construction, agriculture and domestic services, while Central Europeans tend to work in the services and hospitality sectors. Secondly, Mexican migrants are younger than Central European migrants. This might be because Mexican migrants spent fewer years in school than migrants from CE. In Mexico, education is mandatory until 14 years of age, while in CE countries, mandatory education lasts up to age 18. Thirdly, Mexican migrants are significantly lower-educated than Central European migrants. The ratios of primary to tertiary education among Mexican and Central European migrants are essentially the inverse of the other: nearly 70 percent of Mexican migrants have a primary education level, compared to 30 percent among CE migrants, and less than 6 percent of Mexican migrants have a tertiary education level, whereas among Central European migrants this figure is in excess of 20 percent (see Table 4.7).

Despite the fact that Mexican migration is dominated by men, Mexican male and female migrants are both younger than Central European male and female migrants – the 15–24 age cohort is almost 10 percent higher among Mexican than among CE migrants, as the figures for Polish migrants below illustrate (Table 4.8).

The distribution of education among migrating populations of Mexicans and Poles are the inverse of these groups' age distribution: the percentage of migrating Poles with tertiary education is four times higher than the corresponding figure for Mexicans among male migrants and three times higher among women. Around 70 percent of Mexican female and male migrants have primary education, compared to approximately 30 percent of Polish female and male migrants.

Table 4.7 Characteristics of immigrants living in OECD countries by region of origin

Region of origin	Men	Women	Total	Young (15–24)	Primary education	Tertiary education	Employed
Mexico	4 633 000	3 695 000	8 329 000	21.0%	69.6%	5.0%	54.4%
EU 10*	1 684 000	2 068 000	3 752 000	9.4%	32.6%	22.0%	48.8%

*The 10 countries that joined the EU in 2004: Cyprus the Czech Republic Estonia Hungary Latvia Lithuania Malta Poland Slovakia and Slovenia.
Source: cf. OECD (2008).

Table 4.8 Age and gender distribution of the foreign born population [in per cent]

Country of birth	Men (15–24)	Men (25–64)	Men (65+)	Women (15–24)	Women (25–64)	Women (65+)	Total (15–24)	Total (25–64)	Total (65+)
Mexico	23.7	72.7	3.6	19.6	74.5	5.9	21.9	73.5	4.6
Poland	12.7	66.3	21.0	10.2	66.6	23.3	11.3	66.5	22.2

*Data for Slovakia and Lithuania are not included in these statistics of 50 main origin countries in the OECD area.
Source: cf. OECD (2008).

Table 4.9 Educational attainment of the foreign born population [in per cent]

Country of birth	Men Primary	Men Secondary	Men Tertiary	Women Primary	Women Secondary	Women Tertiary	Total Primary	Total Secondary	Total Tertiary
Mexico	70.6	24.2	5.2	68.3	25.4	6.4	69.6	24.7	5.7
Poland	27.7	49.3	23.0	34.2	45.5	20.3	31.3	47.2	21.5

*Data for Slovakia and Lithuania are not included in these statistics of 50 main origin countries in the OECD area.
Source: cf. OECD (2008).

Comparing duration of stay, Polish migrants – taken to be illustrative for Central Europeans as a whole – stay abroad longer than Mexicans. The majority of Poles (80 percent) stay abroad for more than 10 years, both men and women; among Mexican migrants, slightly over half remain abroad for more than a decade. One in four Mexican migrants stay abroad for less than five years, and nearly one in five stay between five and 10 years. The differences between Poles and Mexicans have to do with the EU enlargement in May 2004, as mentioned at the beginning of this chapter, as this made it possible for migrants from Poland to stay and work in EU and EEA countries for unlimited periods, allowing them also to bring or start families abroad. The shorter stays observed among Mexicans have to do with the restrictions imposed by American immigration policy.

Looking at the distribution of the duration of stay abroad by level of education among Mexican and Polish migrant populations, what stands out is that migrants staying abroad for longer than 10 years are the largest group among all levels of education. In the Mexican group, the highest percentage – 62 percent – is among migrants with tertiary education. These are usually professionals with work visas. In the Polish population the difference between levels of education and the length of stay abroad are tiny, at the level of 1 percent.

The Mexican and Polish migrant populations have a similar status in the labour market in terms of total employment, which stands at nearly 55 percent for both populations, as well as total unemployment (around 6 percent) and total inactive migrants (around 40 percent). The biggest differences in relation to labour market status are found when the figures are split according to gender. Employment is higher among male Mexican migrants than among the Polish (67 and 61 percent, respectively), while Polish migrant females have a higher employment percentage than Mexicans (47 and 39 percent, respectively). Inactivity is also higher among Mexican than among than Polish migrant women (55 and 47 percent), and higher among Polish migrant men than among their Mexican counterparts.

The highest rates of employment per level of education are found among migrants with tertiary education; this is the case among both the Mexican and Polish migrant populations. The biggest differences are among migrants with primary education: one in two Mexican migrants are employed; among Polish migrants, one in three.

The employment status per level of education is also reflected in the statistics about sectors of activity of migrant populations.

The biggest differences are visible in producer services – the percentage of Polish migrants employed in this sector is three times higher than for Mexican migrants. A difference of 10 percent can also be observed in the sector of agriculture and industry: 43.5 percent among Mexicans,

Table 4.10 Duration of stay of the foreign born population, by gender [in per cent]

Country of birth	Men 0–5 y	Men 5–10 y	Men 10+ y	Women 0–5 y	Women 5–10 y	Women 10+ y	Total 0–5 y	Total 5–10 y	Total 10+ y
Mexico	26.6	17.5	55.9	22.5	19.8	57.7	24.8	18.5	56.7
Poland	6.1	13..5	80.4	7.4	15.8	76.8	6.8	14.8	78.4

* Data for Slovakia and Lithuania are not included in these statistics of 50 main origin countries in the OECD area.
Source: cf. OECD (2008)

Table 4.11 Duration of stay of the foreign born population, by educational level [in per cent]

Country of birth	Primary 0–5 y	Primary 5–10 y	Primary 10+ y	Secondary 0–5 y	Secondary 5–10 y	Secondary 10+ y	Tertiary 0–5 y	Tertiary 5–10 y	Tertiary 10+ y
Mexico	25.4	18.9	55.7	23.2	18.5	58.3	23.7	14.3	62.0
Poland	6.2	14.4	79.4	6.6	15.5	77.9	7.1	14.6	78.3

* Data for Slovakia and Lithuania are not included in these statistics of 50 main origin countries in the OECD area.
Source: cf. OECD (2008)

Table 4.12 Labour force status of the foreign born population [in per cent]

Country of birth	Men Employed	Men Un-employed	Men In-active	Women Employed	Women Un-employed	Women In-active	Total Employed	Total Un-employed	Total In-active
Mexico	66.9	5.4	27.7	38.7	6.0	55.3	54.4	5.7	39.9
Poland	60.8	7.4	31.9	47.1	5.6	47.3	53.1	6.4	40.5

* Data for Slovakia and Lithuania are not included in these statistics of 50 main origin countries in the OECD area.
Source: cf. OECD (2008).

Table 4.13 Labour market status of the foreign born population by education level [in per cent]

Country of birth	Employed with primary education	Employed with secondary education	Employed with tertiary	Total Employed	Total Unemployed	Total Inactive
Mexico	50.7	61.7	67.6	54.4	5.7	39.9
Poland	31.7	60.3	69.8	53.4	6.4	40.2

*Data for Slovakia and Lithuania are not included in these statistics of 50 main origin countries in the OECD area.
Source: cf. OECD (2008).

Table 4.14 Sectors of activity of the foreign born population, in per cent of the employed population aged 15+ [in per cent]

Country of birth	Agriculture and industry	Producer services	Distributive services	Personal and social services
Mexico	43.5	3.8	15.4	37.3
Poland	33.2	12.6	17.9	36.3

*Data for Slovakia and Lithuania are not included in these statistics of 50 main origin countries in the OECD area.
Source: cf. OECD (2008).

compared 33 percent for Poles. The differences are much smaller in distributive services (15 and 18 percent, respectively) and in personal and social services, where the two groups differ just 1 percent.

Naturally, the numbers analysed in this chapter ultimately describe real people, therefore in the next chapter we will be recounting their migration stories and the effect these experiences had on their human capital formation.

Summary and discussion

The purpose of this chapter was to present the socio-demographic profiles of two groups of migrants from different sides of the world, Central Europeans and Mexicans. In this chapter, we analysed their formal human capital, specifically their level of education, qualifications and status in the labour market, in relation to their demographic characteristics – age, gender and duration of stay. These profiles were discussed in the historical contexts of

Mexican and Central European migration flows (both leaving and returning), with Poland, Slovakia and Lithuania as the case countries for the Central European region.

The choice was made to focus on returnees to Mexico and Central Europe in this chapter because they are the exemplary ones who are able to remit informal human capital. The increased volume and diversity of global return migration since the mid-1990s (Hagan and Wassink, 2020) puts the two groups of migrants analysed at the heart of this book. In the passage below, Hazán (2017) raises many relevant questions relating to return migration which justifies the research findings presented in this book.

> Going beyond the reasons for return, there are a number of major questions for which we have only limited hints. We do not know very well what happens to them once they are back to their origins. Do they return to where they lived before emigrating, or do they go somewhere else? Do they change occupations? Do they use their skills acquired abroad, their experiences in foreign employment and business? Do they pursue opportunities in the formal economy or are they forced to remain in the informal economy where most of them worked before emigrating? Do they bring back capital (savings and other assets)? Do they invest? If so, how? If not, why not? Did their emigration experience change their perceptions of how society does, or might, work? How does their full emigration experience affect their reintegration back in their origins? Do they want to remain in their origins or do they want to return to their destinations? What are the factors that are compelling them or may compel them to stay in their origins? And what are the factors that may compel or are compelling them to re-emigrate to their destinations.
>
> (cf. Hazán, 2017: 5)

In their reflections on an integrated future research agenda (Hagan and Wassink, 2020) recommend, among other things, to produce more comparative and longitudinal studies on returnees, the formation, remitting and mobilisation of their human capital, next to their financial assets and social capital resources. The following chapters, Chapter 5 and Chapter 6, seek to address this knowledge gap.

Notes

1 The principle of free movement of workers is enshrined in Article 45 of the Treaty on the Functioning of the European Union (TFEU). The Treaty rules on free movement of persons initially applied only to economically active persons (i.e. employed persons and jobseekers). In 1993, the Maastricht Treaty gave

new life to the EU rules on free movement of persons, enshrining the Article 20 right of EU citizenship and giving, in Article 21, all EU citizens and their family members the right, in principle, to move and reside freely within the EU. Directive 2004/38/EC on the right of citizens of the Union and their family members to move and reside freely within the territory of the Member States27.The Directive codified previous legislation which dealt separately with distinct categories of EU citizens. The specific rights concerning free movement of workers and their family members are provided in Regulation (EU) No 492/2011 (replacing Regulation (EC) No 1612/68). Accordingly, all Union citizens and their family members have the right to move and reside freely within the territory of the Member States. Directive 2015/54/EU on measures facilitating the exercise of rights conferred on workers in the context of freedom of movement for workers aims at ensuring a more effective and uniform application of the right to free movement and provides specific rules for effective enforcement (Fries-Tersch et al., 2020: 15).

2 Please refer to https://www.oecd.org/about/members-and-partners/.

3 "XII Censo General de Poblacin y Vivienda, 2000" by the national institute of statistics (Instituto National de Estadistica Geografia y Informatica INEGI).

4 https://mimy.eurice.eu/projects/dissemination/issues; https://www.pewresearch.org/hispanic/2009/02/12/unemployment-rose-sharply-among-latino-immigrants-in-2008/.

5 Encuesta Nacional de Ocupación y Empleo; the Mexican Census, and the National Survey of Employment and Occupation.

6 See also: Juan Luis Diaz Ordaz. *Perfil Socioeconómico y de Reinserción Laboral de los Migrantes Mexicanos de Retorno: Análisis Comparativo entre 2005–2007 y 2008–2012.*

7 The populations of the three countries in 1990 were: Poland: 38 183 000; Lithuania: 3 698 000; Slovakia: 5 299 187.

8 The 10 countries that joined the EU in 2004 were Cyprus, the Czech Republic, Estonia, Hungary, Latvia, Lithuania, Malta, Poland, Slovakia and Slovenia.

9 A portmanteau of "British" or "Britain" and "exit". The term "Brexit" refers to the withdrawal of the United Kingdom (UK) from the European Union (EU) and the European Atomic Energy Community (EAEC or Euratom) at midnight on 31 January 2020 CET. To date, the UK is the first and only country to have formally left the EU, after 47 years of membership. Before that, the UK was a member of the EU's predecessor, the European Communities (EC), having joined on 1 January 1973. The country continued to participate in the European Union Customs Union and European Single Market during a transition period that ended on 31 December 2020. https://videohive.net/item/uk-flag-and-eu-flag-on-retro-tvs-brexit-concept-/24765426

10 Return mobility is a type of long-term labour mobility, where EU movers return to their country of origin. Due to the lack of precise figures, return mobility is approximated from figures of nationals moving to their country of citizenship (Fries-Tersch et al., 2018: 18).

11 *CEEYouth: The comparative study of young migrants from Poland and Lithuania in the context of Brexit*, Grant No. 393464; from the text of the application.

References

Abel, G. J. and Sander, N. (2014). Quantifying global international migration flows. *Science*, 343 (6178): 1520–1522. doi:10.1126/science.1248676.

Anacka, M. (2010). Poakcesyjni migranci powrotni w Badaniu Aktywności Eko-
nomicznej Ludności. In I. Grabowska-Lusińska (ed.), *Poakcesyjne powroty
Polaków. CMR Working Papers*, 43(101), 13–26.

Barcevičius, E. (2016). How Successful are Highly Qualified Return Migrants in
the Lithuanian Labour Market? *International Migration*, 54(3), 35–47.

Barcevičius, E. and Žvalionyte, D. (eds.) (2012). *Užburtas ratas? Lietuvos gyven-
toju grįžtamoji ir pakartotine migracija*. Vilnius: Vaga.

Barcevičius, E. and Žvalionyte, D. (eds.) (2015). Savi ar svetimi? Grįžusiu
migrantu integracija I darbo rinką ir visuomenę. *Politologija, specialusis
numeris*, 2, 3–169.

Camp, R.A. (1993). *Politics in Mexico*. New York: Oxford University Press.

Caponi, V. (2006). Heterogeneous human capital and migration: who migrates
from Mexico to the US? IZA Discussion Papers, No. 2446, Institute for the
Study of Labor (IZA), Bonn.

Fihel, A., Kaczmarczyk, P., Okólski, M., and Krzaklewska, E. (2007). *Migracje
"nowych Europejczyków"– teraz i przedtem*. Warszawa: Wydawnictwa Uni-
wersytetu Warszawskiego.

Fries-Tersch, E., Tugran, T., & Bradley, H. (2018). 2017 Annual Report on Intra-
EU Labour Mobility. *European Commission*, 12.

Fries-Tersch, E., Jones, M., Bock, B., de Keyser, L., and Tugran, T. (2020). 2020
Annual Report on Intra-EU Mobility. Brussels: European Commission, Directo-
rate General for Employment, Social Affairs and Inclusion.

Gonzalez-Barrera, A. (2015). *More Mexicans leaving than coming to the US*.
Washington: Pew Research Center.

Hagan, J. M., Hernández-León, R. and Demonsant, J. L. (2015). *Skills of the
unskilled: Work and mobility among Mexican migrants*. California: University of
California Press.

Hagan, J. M. and Wassink, J. T. (2016). New skills, new jobs: Return migration,
skill transfers, and business formation in Mexico. *Social Problems*, 63 (4): 513–
533. doi:10.1093/socpro/spw021.

Hagan, J. M. and Wassink, J. T. (2020). Return migration around the world: An
integrated agenda for future research. *Annual Review of Sociology*, 46, 533–552.

Hagan, J. M., Wassink, J. T. , and Castro, B. (2019). A longitudinal analysis of
resource mobilization among forced and voluntary return migrants in Mexico.
Journal of Ethnic and Migration Studies, 45(1), 170–189.

Hanson, G. H. (2009). The economic consequences of the international migration
of labor. *Annual Review of Economics*, 1(1), 179–208.

Hazán, M. (2017). Understanding return migration to Mexico: Towards a comprehensive policy for the reintegration of returning migrants. https://ccis.ucsd.edu/_
files/wp193.pdf.

Hazans, M. (2008). Post-enlargement return migrants' earnings premium: Evidence
from Latvia. doi:10.2139/ssrn.1269728.

Iara, A. (2008). Skill diffusion by temporary migration? Returns to Western European work experience in Central and East European countries (No. 46). WIIW
Working Paper.

72   Population characteristics of migrants

Iglicka, K. (2009). *Powroty Polaków w okresie kryzysu gospodarczego. W pętli pułapki migracyjnej.* Warszawa: Scholar.

Illés, S. (2004). Foreigners in Hungary: migration from the European Union. Working papers on population, family and welfare. No. 5. Budapest: Hungarian Demographic Research Institute.

Kindler, M. (2018). Poland's Perspective on the Intra-European Movement of Poles. Implications and Governance Responses. In *Between Mobility and Migration* (183–204). Cham: Springer.

Klimavičiūtė, L., Parutis, V., Jonavičienė, D., Karolak, M., and Wermińska-Wiśnicka, I. (2020). The Impact of Brexit on Young Poles and Lithuanians in the UK: Reinforced Temporariness of Migration Decisions. *Central Eastern European Migration Review*, 9(1), 127–142.

Kochhar, R. (2008). Latino Labor Report 2008: Construction Reverses Job Growth for Latinos. Washington, D.C.: Pew Hispanic Center.

Lang, T. and Nadler, R. (2014). Return migration to Central and Eastern Europe: transnational migrants' perspectives and local businesses' needs. (Forum IfL, 23). Leipzig: Leibniz-Institut für Länderkunde e.V. (IfL). https:// nbn-resolving. org/urn:nbn:de:0168-ssoar-390656.

Lulle, A., King, R., Dvorakova, V., & Szkudlarek, A. (2019). Between disruptions and connections: "New" European Union migrants in the United Kingdom before and after the Brexit. *Population, Space and Place*, 25(1), e2200.

Martin, R. and Radu, D. (2012). Return Migration: The Experience of Eastern Europe 1. *International Migration*, 50(6), 109–128.

Masferrer, C. and Roberts, B. R. (2012). Going back home? Changing demography and geography of Mexican return migration, *Population Research and Policy Review*, 31(4), 465–496.

Masferrer, C. and Roberts, B. (2012). Going Back Home? Changing Demography and Geography of Mexican Return Migration. *Population Research Policy Review*, 31, 472.

Massey, D. S., Arango, J., Hugo, G., Kouaouci, A., Pellegrino, A., and Taylor, J. E. (1993). Theories of international migration: A review and appraisal. *Population and Development Review*, 19(3), 431–466.

Massey, D. S., Durand, J., and Pren, K. (2016). Why border enforcement backfired American. *Journal of Sociology,* 121(5),1557–1600.

Massey, D. S. and Espinosa, K. E. (1997). What's driving Mexico-U.S. migration? A theoretical, empirical, and policy analysis. *American Journal of Sociology*, 102(4), 939–999.

Massey, D. S. and Parrado, E. A. (1998). International migration and business formation in Mexico. *Social Science Quarterly*, 79(1), 1–20.

Ordaz Díaz, J. L., & Li Ng, J. J. (2016). Perfil socioeconómico y de inserción laboral de los migrantes mexicanos de retorno: análisis comparativo entre 2005–2007 y 2008–2012. *Nuevas experiencias de la migración de retorno.*

Organisation for Economic Co-operation and Development (2008). *A profile of immigrant populations in the 21st century: data from OECD countries.* Paris: OECD.

Parrado, E. A. and Gutierrez, E. Y. (2016). The changing nature of return migration to Mexico, 1990–2010. *Sociology of Development*, 2(2), 93–118. doi:10.1525/sod.2016.2.2.9.

Passel, J. S., D'Vera Cohn, G. B. A., Gonzalez-Barrera, A., and Center, P. H. (2012). *Net migration from Mexico falls to zero – and perhaps less*. Washington, DC: Pew Hispanic Center.

Pollard, N., Latorre, M., and Sriskandarajah, D. (2008). Floodgates or turnstiles?: Post-EU enlargement migration flows to (and from) the UK. Institute for Public Policy Research.

Szymańska, J., Ulasiński, C., and Bieńkowska, D. (2012). "Zaraz wracam… albo i nie": skala powrotów, motywacje i strategie życiowe reemigrantów z województwa śląskiego. *Studia Migracyjne-Przegląd Polonijny*, 38(3), 145.

Villarreal, A. (2014). Explaining the decline in Mexico-U.S. migration: The effect of the great recession. *Demography*, 51(6): 2203–2228. doi:10.1007/s13524–13014–0351–0354.

Waddell, B. J. and Fontenla, M. (2015). The Mexican Dream? The effect of return migrants on hometown development. *The Social Science Journal*, 52(3), 386–396. doi:10.1016/j.soscij.2015.02.003.

Wassink, J. (2020). International migration experience and entrepreneurship: Evidence from Mexico. *World Development*, 136, 105077.

Wassink, J. T. and Hagan, J. M. (2018). A dynamic model of self-employment and socioeconomic mobility among return migrants: The case of urban Mexico. *Social Forces*, 96(3), 1069–1096.

Wassink, J. T. and Hagan, J. M. (2020). How local community context shapes labour market re-entry and resource mobilization among return migrants: An examination of rural and urban communities in Mexico. *Journal of Ethnic and Migration Studies*.doi:10.1080/1369183X.2020.1758552.

Žvalionyte, D. (2014). *Grįžusiųjų migrantų integracija kilmes šalies darbo rinkoje: Lietuvos atvejo analize*. Daktaro disertacija. Vilnius: Vilniaus universiteto leidykla, PhD Dissertation.

5 Acquisition of informal human capital through migration

Introduction

As Janta et al. (2019: 1742–1743) rightly point out, it is worth studying "(...) migration as a vehicle for skill acquisition, employment and employability". This chapter is about acquisition, development and enhancement of Migration-Impacted Informal Human Capital (MigCap), corresponding with Stage 1 of the analytical model presented in Chapter 3. The analysis presented on the pages of this chapter will be conducted at multiple levels – macro (big picture), meso (cross-case) and micro (vignette, testimonials, cases) – juxtaposing Mexican and Central European data sources, both quantitative and qualitative.

In short, this analysis will create a multi-level, interdisciplinary, mixed-method analysis of the impact of international migration on the various components of informal human capital that were defined in Chapter 2: mind skills, soft skills, maker skills and life skills.

From a neoclassical perspective, the acquisition and development of informal human capital can be regarded as an investment, where resources are gathered in order to obtain deferred effects in the future (Green, 2011). Hagan, Hernández-León and Demonsant (2015: 22) consider the acquisition of skills in migration contexts as "a lifelong process, happening in workplaces, families, communities, through migrant careers". The authors emphasize that the models of human capital should not only focus on a narrow set of variables, but should take into account the fact that acquiring skills is a social process. They also claim that the acquisition of soft skills as a result of international migration is broadly related to the formation, strengthening and development of total human capital.

One of the social space where migrants can acquire MigCap is a space of an organization, an institution, a workplace (cf. Grabowska, 2018; Haynes and Galasińska, 2016). However, not every organizational environment and job content is conducive to the reinforcement of informal

DOI: 10.4324/9781003011545-5

human capital. MigCap is developed mainly in relational social spaces (Donati and Archer, 2015; Shan, 2013), i.e., spaces where people can communicate with each other, establish relationships, observe each other, learn by doing things together and collaborate. The workplace is a socially meaningful space in which persons experience relational, reflexive socialization (Archer, 2015). When a workplace isolates a person and they are unable to interact with other people, it is not conducive to social learning. However, even under these circumstances, it remains difficult to unambiguously gauge the exact extent and orientation (positive or negative) of the effects on social learning, because even while isolated, a person can reflexively observe the social world around them, from a distance, under a uniform, as a so-called mid-sider – a person who is both an insider and somewhat of an outsider at the same time.

When migrants find themselves in a new organization or an institution, a new workplace in a foreign country, in a different culture, where people speak a different language, they experience a discontinuity of context, which may cause them to experience surprise, "aha moments" and stimulate reflexivity (Grabowska, 2018). At that time they begin to notice the similarities and differences between the world around them, and become aware of their own possibilities and limitations. Migrants record, recode and respond to new experiences in a new socio-cultural context. The experience of working abroad makes it possible to confront the socialization effects of one's sending country with the surrounding social world of the receiving country.

The most effective acquisition of MigCap occurs when people are forced to reflect on their position in a given situation (Jarvis, 2007). Habermas (1992) talks about problematic situations that force us to renegotiate our previous behaviour and social practices. Thus, such context changes, especially as they occur in migration, favour the acquisition of soft skills. Context may be fragmentary and random, but it also strengthens the informal human capital that a migrant already has (e.g. because they worked in a similar environment and under similar conditions in their home country).

The acquisition of new components of MigCap occurs when people find themselves in a new, different context, in which they are required to respond to various social situations and stimuli. Some people, however, do not answer, and then the development of MigCap is obstructed. This may occur in situations where, for example, a person switches to a completely different sector or industry and takes a job with a completely different work content, going abroad only to earn, not to earn and learn. This was the case with many post-accession migrants from Poland, Slovakia and Lithuania. Further on in this chapter we will take a closer look at these migrants who did not acquire soft skills.

Next to the accidental acquisition of MigCap mentioned above, there is also a motivated acquisition (Jarvis, 2007). This occurs when people experience a change in socio-cultural context and want (for not all people do) to learn the organisational culture, rules, codes of practices and practices in a new workplace.

The instances of not acquiring MigCap are alienation and anomie. These occur when the difference in socio-cultural contexts is so great that a person – in the context of this discussion, a migrant – is unable to respond to it and alienates themselves, potentially even becoming homeless and becoming involved in crime. Examples of this were found among the Polish migrants studied in *The Polish Peasant in Europe and America* (Thomas and Znaniecki, 1996: 1920–22) and among post-accession migrants from Poland (Garapich, 2014).

> (…) migration may constitute 'significant learning moments' for individuals (…) But migration can also be a stultifying experience, with poor learning content".
>
> (Williams, 2007: 374)

It is worth noting that temporary, seasonal jobs are less conducive to social learning than places where stays of more than three months – more than a single season – are possible. Post-accession migrants from Poland, Slovakia and Lithuania had been extending their stays since at least 2005, which also resulted in longer stays in a given workplace. They do not acquire soft skills in the same way as short-stay migrants due to different patterns of interaction with the host society. Levitt (2001) identified several patterns of interaction that we were also able to identify in migrant workplaces: (1) the recipient observer, (2) the instrumental adopter, and (3) the goal-oriented innovator (purposeful innovator). These patterns can be combined with the social forms of learning discussed above, and this combination helps to explain the various effects of the acquisition, enhancement and transfer of social competences. Introducing the concept of social remittances into the sociology of migration, Levitt (1998) said that migrants who have more opportunities to interact with the host society are more reflexive about their social practices than those who are only superficial observers surrounding reality. This applies especially to those who are locked down in their ethnic enclaves.

In order to be able to function in the modern world, we must learn all the time. Migration, through changes in socio-cultural contexts, creates opportunities for informal learning, and fosters reflexive socialization throughout life (Archer, 2015). As migrants spend most of their time in workplaces, it is workplaces that become sources of surprises and adaptation to changes (Grabowska, 2018). Such social learning is a reflection on practical experience in the culture of a given workplace and in the social world of its participants (Evans et al., 2004).

Engaging in international migration, mostly into work and education, does not automatically lead to the acquisition of MigCap. Nevertheless, migration situations may favour social learning (Williams, 2007), including the aforementioned surprises and "aha moments" (Grabowska, 2018) that facilitate the acquisition and strengthening of universal, transferable skills (Williams and Baláž, 2005; Grabowska, 2018).

Williams (2007) and Hagan at al. (2015) argue that neither unskilled migrants nor migrants who work in unskilled jobs experience a social vacuum in social learning. On the contrary, even in simple jobs people learn new skills. Research on the tacit dimensions (cf. Polanyi, 2009; Williams, 2007) of migration experiences related to social learning and experiencing the social world abroad considers precisely the acquisition, strengthening, development and transfer of soft skills (Grabowska, 2018).

MigCap can be formed in various domains of life; the process of its informal acquisition takes place primarily in the workplace and in the local community (Green, 2011). The workplace is one of the most important settings for social learning (Wenger, 1998). The acquisition of MigCap in the workplace usually takes place through interactions between people (Marsick and Watkins, 2001) and the relationships they build (Donati and Archer, 2015). People learn through experience and cooperation, especially when the task to be performed is interpersonal and relational. The acquisition of MigCap can be a by-product of broader learning processes. Workplaces in general, and in particular in the context of migration, are the result of economic and organisational models, work customs, industrial relations and organisational culture (Haynes and Galasińska, 2016; Grabowska, 2018).

The acquisition and development of MigCap can be considered an investment in human capital (Green, 2011; Hagan et al., 2015; Grabowska, 2018). It is worth studying not only the process of acquiring MigCap, but also the determinants of this process, related to contacts with representatives of the host society and other migrants. International migrants might learn through: observation (Levitt, 2001), communication (Lundvall and Johnson, 1994), experiencing and performing tasks, and undertaking various activities together with other people (Arrow, 1962). Capacity for learning was defined in the conceptual chapter as mind skills – cognitive skills – one of the components of informal human capital affected by international migration.

> There are areas of unusual learning, places where perspectives meet and new possibilities arise. Radically new insights often arise at the boundaries.
>
> (Williams, 2007: 367)

Through international migration, people learn how to use opportunities, gain respect, recognition and other matters that relate to the wellbeing of an individual (Monteith and Giesbert, 2017). Learning is not restricted to elite movers: it is accessible to everyone (cf. Morosanu at al., 2019).

In the following, we present our findings on the acquisition of MigCap and the obstruction thereof among Mexican and Central European migrants from a multi-level perspective: macro (big picture), meso (cross-case) and micro (vignettes, testimonials) although the data is not evenly available for Mexicans and Central Europeans.

Big picture

The macro-level perspective or "big picture" of the acquisition and enhancement of informal human capital through migration is based on the available statistical data sources. As the term "macro" implies, this section does not deal with details of the impact of international migration on informal human capital, but seeks to outline a background for the qualitative insights presented in the subsequent sections. As such, this section is about inquiring into the magnitude of the impact of migration on informal human capital.

In the following, we juxtapose various quantitative, statistical data relating to the selected Central European countries (Poland, Lithuania and Slovakia) and Mexico in six tables (Tables 5.1–5.6). The data presented below is not comparable with each other due to the different methods (face-to-face questionnaires and online surveys) and research tools used; the manner in which the questions were formulated and presented also differed between the various questionnaires. The studies used in this book were also conducted at different points in time between 2004 and 2020.

The acquisition of MigCap is measured in four ways. The first is based on the percentages of the answers in the sample and cross-tabbed with gender, education and duration of migration. The second is based on a rating scale (Likert scale) used to gauge migrants' acquisition of various components of MigCap through statements to which they could respond with "strongly agree", "agree", "neutral", "disagree", or "strongly disagree". The third is based on the acquisition index, and the fourth is based on the regression model.

The selected studies presented below describe migrants, predominantly returnees. Analysing these various data sources and results, one can notice a number of commonalities.

Firstly, the top-rated informal human capital component acquired and enhanced by migrants relates to mind skills – English/foreign language and communication skills, except in the latest study among Slovaks (Baláž at al., 2019), where the ability to deal with new challenges dominates; this might have to do with the age of the respondents in this survey, which focused on young adults between the ages of 18 and 29.

Secondly, soft skills – teamwork and work experience – are highly appreciated as a MigCap acquisition, along with self-confidence and resilience to stress. The latter two, especially, form part of the PsyCap (Psychological Capital) and COR (Conservation of Resources) discussed in Chapter 2 of this book.

Thirdly, soft skills such as learning new approaches to work, new management techniques and methods of organisation, showing initiative, the ability to experiment and showing work practice gained through migration are also evaluated by migrants and returnees as important.

Fourthly, maker skills are also not evenly asked in all these data sources. They are mostly pronounced among Mexican migrants.

Table 5.1 shows the most important findings for the processes of learning skills by Mexicans in the USA from the perspective of returnees. They nearly equally cherish on-the-job training and instructions from the boss or co-workers and observation, social interaction with co-workers, experimentation and practice (Hagan et al., 2015). We are not going to relate here to any gender difference due to the fact that the sample is biased towards male and the sample is too limited for women. Mexican migrants particularly cherish the acquisition of skills and reskilling in the US labour market – 81 percent of returnees reported these acquisitions (Hagan, Demonsant and Chávez, 2014).

In the catalogue of social skills acquired as a result of migration in informal ways (cf. Table 5.1. work in the USA) identified in the Mexican

Table 5.1 Social contexts and processes of learning and acquiring skills in the United States by Mexican returnees [in per cent]

Learning process	*Total* N= *162*	*Male* n= *143*	*Female* n= *19*
Formal (institutional) Vocational training and other schooling leading to credentials	7	8	0
Formal (workplace) On-the-job training program designed by workplace or explicit instruction from boss or co-workers	56	49	68
Informal (work) Observation, social interaction with co-workers, experimentation and practice	57	57	53

Source: cf. Hagan et al. (2015: 109, Table 4.2).

research one can enumerate: skills relating to serving customers, new attitudes towards work, new work routines, e.g. being on time, entrepreneurial skills linked mostly to an initiative, thinking and acting in an entrepreneurial way, self-confidence, skills connected to leading a team or a task, teamwork, work process (cf. Hagan et al., 2015: 32). The acquisition of these soft skills depend however on occupational settings and an experienced change between origin and destination by a migrant.

The most recent findings (DAINA CEEYouth, 2020) of the comparative study among returnees to two Central European countries (Poland and Lithuania) are presented in Table 5.2. As discussed in the first part of this chapter, English language skills are considered the most important migratory acquisition by both of these groups. The second most important skill was resilience to stress among Lithuanians, teamwork among Polish migrants. More Lithuanians than Poles developed leadership skills and the ability to show initiative. On the other hand, more Poles than Lithuanians developed entrepreneurship skills while abroad. This might have to do with the general high rates of entrepreneurship in the population of Poland since the 1990s.

Among both Polish and Lithuanian migrants, the majority of the mind and soft components of informal human capital listed in Table 5.2 is best acquired and developed through a medium-duration stay abroad, between five and 10 years. These include teamwork, leadership skills, resilience to stress and entrepreneurship in the case of Lithuanians. However, some soft skills require more time; one example of such a skill is entrepreneurship, where 10 years spent abroad are more important than five. On the other hand, duration of stay was less important for language skills – staying and working abroad for any period exceeding one year was shown to affect language acquisition and the development of communication skills.

The *Migratory Skill Acquisition Index* was created by summarising the six types of soft skills included in the survey question: "Which of the following skills have you developed while working in Great Britain?" The respondents could select the following mind and soft skills: teamwork, leadership skills, knowledge of English, resilience to stress, entrepreneurship, and taking initiative. Migrants more often acquired interpersonal soft skills, such as language skills or teamwork, than intrapersonal ones, e.g. resilience to stress or showing initiative.

While analysing the acquisition of individual soft skills by citizens of Poland and Lithuania, we found that a significantly higher percentage of Lithuanians acquired leadership skills (41.3 percent; PL=27.1 percent) and the ability to show initiative (LT=46.1 percent; PL=32.8 percent).

Table 5.2 Acquisition of skills by Polish and Lithuanian returnees (multiple choice question)

	PL		LT	
	n	%	n	%
Knowledge of English	323	62.6	130	63.1
Teamwork	248	48.1	107	51.9
Stress resilience	195	37.8	85	41.3
Taking the initiative	169	32.8	95	46.1
Leadership skills	140	27.1	85	41.3
Entrepreneurship	126	24.4	45	21.8

*Formulation of the survey question: Which of the following skills have you developed while working in the UK?
The comparative Polish-Lithuarian survey with return migrants conducted in May–July 2020 within the DAINA CEEYouth; total PL n=516; LT n=206; only completed questionnaires.
Source: Author's elaboration.

The Migratory Skill Acquisition Index ranges from 0 to 6, where 0 means that a person has not acquired any of the skills listed in the survey, and 6 means that he has acquired all of them. Slightly over 67 percent of Poles and 64 percent of Lithuanians declared that they had acquired at least one of the six mind and soft skills mentioned. More than 30 percent of Poles and 35 percent of Lithuanians did not acquire any of these six informal skills. This will be analysed in detail in the next section of this chapter, which is devoted to the obstruction of MigCap development.

The acquisition of mind and soft skills was lower among Polish migrants (M=2.33; SD=2.08) than Lithuanians (M=2.66; SD=2.31). The difference is significant at the level of the statistical trend t (344.96) =1.773; p=0.073.

Using multiple regression analysis (see Table 5.4), we investigated which factors described from the perspective of the domains of life related to the concept of conservation of resources presented in Chapter 2 (work, education, housing, relations), were important to predict the Migratory Skill Acquisition Index. We found that 37.8 percent of the Acquisition Index variability can be predicted on the basis of these variables. The most important factor determining soft skill level is employment (B=1.798; p<0.001). People who have a job acquire more soft skills than unemployed or inactive people, which proves the arguments presented at the beginning of this chapter about workplaces as significant, relational and meaningful environments for the acquisition of MigCap. Another factor determining the level of mind and soft skill acquisition is the duration of migration. People

Table 5.3 Migration Skill Acquisition Index for Polish and Lithuanians migrants

	PL		LT	
	n	%	n	%
0	166	32.2	73	35.4
1	51	9.9	8	3.9
2	57	11.0	14	6.8
3	75	14.5	21	10.2
4	77	14.9	31	15.0
5	37	7.2	30	14.6
6	53	10.3	29	14.1
M	2.33		2.66	
Me	2.08		2.31	
Mo	0.33		0.06	
SD	-1.21		-1.57	
Min	0.00		0.00	
Max	6.00		6.00	

The comparative Polish-Lithuanian survey with return migrants conducted in May–July 2020 within the DAINA CEEYouth; total PL n=516; LT n=206; only completed questionnaires.
Source: Author's elaboration.

who have been abroad for more than five years have a higher index than migrants who remain abroad for shorter periods.

Because Poland is the largest country in Central Europe, more data sources are available on the acquisition and development of informal human capital through migration than for the other countries under study in this book.

At least two Slovakian studies were conducted by Williams and Baláž and co-authors in 2005 and 2019 with similar sets of questions (see Tables 5.5 and 5.6).

Although language skills were the most highly-rated form of human capital acquired as a result of migratory experience among Slovaks in 2005, in 2019, the greatest importance was placed on the ability to deal with new challenges, self-confidence and learning new skills. Also, these skills were more highly rated by women than by men, as well as by people with higher education (see Table 5.6).

The macro picture presented above, based on available samples from available data sources for Mexican and Central European migrants, shows the significance of the acquisition of MigCap through international migration.

Table 5.4 Multiple linear regression model with Migration Skill Acquisition Index for Polish and Lithuanian migrants

	MIGRATION SKILL ACQUISITION INDEX	
	B	SE
Constant	2.334***	1.003
Sex (ref=men) women	-0.393	0.558
Domain 1. Education (ref=other than higher) higher	0.158	0.137
Domain 2. Labour market situation (ref=unemployed) inactive employed	-0.972** 1.798***	0.343 0.311
Domain 3. Housing (ref=own) rent with someone	-0.676 -0.704	0.434 0.433
Domain 4. Relations (ref=no) yes	-0.074	0.710
Return from abroad to the same place (ref=yes) no	0.247	0.236
Time of migration (ref=1–5) 5–10 years more then 10	0.536** 0.543**	0.157 0.162
Adjusted R²	0.378	

*** $p<0.001$; ** $p<0.01$; * $p<0.05$.
The comparative Polish-Lithuanian survey with return migrants conducted in May–July 2020 within the DAINA CEEYouth; total PL n=516; LT n=206; only completed questionnaires.
Source: Author's elaboration.

Table 5.5 Self-assessment of migration experience in various occupational groups of returnees to Slovakia (scale 1–5; where *1=unimportant* and *5=fundamentally important)*

	Profes- sionals n= 64	Students n=55	Au pairs n=67
Acquiring qualifications	2.8	2.8	2.5
Learning new skills	3.5	3.2	3.0
Acquiring new ideas	3.9	4.0	3.1
Ability to deal with new challenges	3.8	4.0	3.9
Learning new approaches to my work	4.0	4.0	3.1
English language ability	4.1	4.6	4.6
Confidence in my abilities	4.0	4.2	4.3
The overall importance for my life	3.4	3.0	3.7

Source: cf. Williams and Baláž (2005: 459; Table 4).

Table 5.6 Self-reported acquisition of human capital acquired by Slovakian current migrants and returnees

Human capital component	Total	Gender		Education		
		Female	Male	Primary	Secondary	Higher
Numbers	366	220	148	6	229	131
Composition	100.00	60.11	39.89	1.64	62.57	35.79
Acquiring formal qualifications	3.25	3.29	3.21	3.51	3.11	3.73
Learning new skills	4.01	4.20	3.84	4.27	3.91	4.34
Ability to deal with new challenges	4.10	4.28	3.93	3.97	4.05	4.36
Self-confidence	4.08	4.27	3.90	3.95	4.00	4.43
Learning a language	3.69	3.94	3.46	4.03	3.57	4.08
Learning to adapt to new cultures	3.71	3.90	3.53	4.47	3.57	4.00

Likert scale: 1=not at all important to 5=very important.
Source: cf. Baláž at al. (2019: 7).

Obstruction

The obstruction of MigCap acquisition is connected here to non-forming, non-mobilising and non-developing informal skills through international migration. This can be caused or exacerbated by migrants' attitudes or external circumstances – e.g. a desire to earn, not learn; not choosing opportunities to establish relationships in the workplace or failing to notice or participate in opportunities for informal learning; stultifying working environments.

Using the data relating to Polish and Lithuanian migrants, we were able to analyse which migrants failed to acquire any MigCap as compared to those who acquired informal human capital. Comparing between the group of migrants who did not acquire any mind and soft skills and the group of migrants that did, one of the first things that stands out is that their MigCap acquisition is higher among Lithuanians and among women. It seems that men, especially Polish men, are more likely to resist the acquisition of informal human capital. People who have spent between one and five years abroad are less likely to acquire MigCap. People who do not acquire MigCap return to their country of origin, mostly to towns and villages, not big cities which obstruct the transfer.

As previously mentioned, not all social spaces are relational and conducive to the type of social learning that leads to the acquisition of informal human capital, and this is particularly true of workplaces. Some working environments

Table 5.7 Comparison of Polish and Lithuanian returnees who acquired / did not acquire soft skills – descriptive statistics

Variable	Value	Not acquired/ obstructed		Acquired	
		n	%	n	%
Country	PL	166	69.5	350	72.5
	LT	73	30.5	133	27.5
Gender	Women	187	78.9	329	69.3
	Men	50	21.1	146	30.7
How many years in GB?	1–5	86	36.0	189	39.1
	5–10	69	28,9	152	31,5
	10<	84	35,1	142	29,4
Perma-nent resi-dence	Moved in and out of the coun-try (min 1 year in the UK)	43	18.0	78	16.1
	Stayed continuously	196	82.0	405	83.9
Back to the same place?	No, but I returned to a city / town of similar size	12	5.0	16	3.3
	No, I returned to a bigger city / town	33	13.8	107	22.2
	No, I returned to a smaller city / town	21	8.8	19	3.9
	Yes	173	72.4	341	70.6
Back to origin country	No, after leaving the UK and before moving to CO I lived in another country	20	8.4	40	8.3
	Yes	219	91.6	443	91.7

The comparative Polish-Lithuanian survey with return migrants conducted in May–July 2020 within the DAINA CEEYouth; total PL n=516; LT n=206; only completed questionnaires. Source: Author's elaboration.

cause social isolation, for example work in fish processing, which requires clothing that covers the entire head and body.

> I worked in a fish processing plant. In the so-called freezer, at the evisceration table, with coverall uniform also covering the head and face. It was cold, foul and humid. I was alone with myself, portioning the fish. It was too cold and smelly to have any conversation. During the breaks, there were other people of colour and from Central and Eastern Europe, but I didn't feel like talking to anyone.
>
> (male migrant from Poland, born in 1988)

As described in *The Polish Peasant in Europe and America* by Thomas and Znaniecki (1996: 1920–1922) such experiences in a host country may lead to alienation and anomie. This can be fostered by seasonal migrants, who do not stay long in any workplace, do not enter into social relations and do not actually desire to learn from the host society. These migrants treat migration only as a source of income, not as a means to gain knowledge ("earn, not learn").

> I went there only to earn money, so that we could live better in Poland. I went for a few months to earn some extra money [at the office]. I can't say that I learned anything new … and I wasn't open to it either.
>
> (male migrant from Poland, born in 1987)

There are also known cases of exploitation and discrimination of migrants by employers in host countries. Such situations may, on the one hand, foster social alienation and encourage xenophobic attitudes, which may obstruct the acquisition of informal human capital; on the other hand, they can also inspire reflexivity, leading migrants to question why people behave this way, and whether is it worth acting or withdrawing.

The obstruction of MigCap acquisition and development through international migration is not unequivocal. By analysing and understanding the causes and forms of such obstructions, one can even more clearly highlight the importance of individual factors in relation to mind and soft skills. The more socio-culturally similar the sending and receiving places are, the fewer the opportunities to learn new skills are. The less relational environments are where interpersonal interactions are limited due to working conditions (temperature, noise, distance) or because of the temporary nature of the employment, the fewer the opportunities to establish relationships and learn through communication and cooperation are. The more unpleasant experiences migrants have gone through during migration (cheating, exploitation, discrimination), the more their acquisition and development of new components of MigCap is obstructed.

Meso and micro pictures

The following sections of this book get qualitative insights into the components of informal human capital identified in the quantitative analyses of the previous section.

Mind and soft skills

Foreign languages, English in particular, have always been highly valued by migrants. International mobility in the EU connected to work and studies helps the learning of a foreign language. Dustman (1999) even refers to it as English "language capital", defining it as an internationalised form of human capital that is flexibly transferable to other locations and appreciated in almost all organisations. As Dustman at al. (2003) demonstrated, there exists a positive relationship between the acquisition of language skills and the achievement of higher employment status and greater earnings. Language gives people the capacity to actively shape the world and to negotiate meanings (Williams, 2007: 370). Learning and developing language and therefore communication skills is a social and cultural event (Baláž and Williams, 2004: 220).

Language and communication skills in a broader conceptual perspective are important in the careers of migrants. Mastering a foreign language not only increases a person's employment opportunities, but also life opportunities relating to self-expression, which results in greater self-confidence and strengthens informal learning processes. Williams and Baláž (2005) found that language skills provided Slovak migrants with instruments of social recognition in various conditions, especially in the workplace. Migrants' language skills allow non-migrants to understand who they are, what they do and how they relate to others, especially those who are different from them in terms of mobility experience. Language skills also strengthen business negotiating opportunities. Furthermore, after a migrant returns to their home country, language skills are a valuable tool that helps improve their situation on the labour market.

During the initial phase of migration, migrants usually practice listening skills, as they must learn the language, to comprehend the local accent and to understand social situations. While there are many great books on how to speak (cf. Cicero's *On the Orator*; Aristotle's *Rhetoric*), we are rarely taught how to listen. We are of course expected to listen at school, but no one teaches us how to listen effectively, in informal situations. Migration therefore presents an excellent opportunity to practice listening skills.

> I think that working in services, sales overseas, on the side of a client, gives the ability to listen to and understand the client. These are very valuable experiences.
>
> (female migrant from Poland, born in 1990)

With regard to the acquisition of informal human capital, it is confirmed that by acquiring and strengthening linguistic skills, a person unlocks social relations, builds self-confidence and can better understand the social world around them. People also become aware of the differences in learning outcomes: formal at school and informal, "real-life", for instance in the workplace, especially abroad.

> (...) when you work with English people who speak foreign languages, you gain such confidence in communicating with them (...) because you are forced to do so. If one does not want to be locked up, forced only to contact Poles, he must go beyond that. Humans have to use this language despite the fact that at first they are embarrassed, you know how everyone else is. Because the language we learn at school has nothing to do with what is then used in England. So, such acquisition of self-confidence in communication.
>
> (female migrant from Poland, small town, born in 1988)

Janta et al. (2019) argue that foreign language skills facilitate not only personal development, but also employability, and help realise occupational utility.

Language can also be a source of self-confidence. It is connected to trusting oneself with understanding a social situation in order to be aware of what is accepted or what is not allowed in a specific culture, or is as a *faux-pas*. Self-confidence is also an important factor in a person's ability and preparedness to "open themselves" towards other people.

> I learnt a language. Yes, it gives self-confidence, openness. Definitely time management, I think it's very [important] because of my lifestyle. Self-organization as well (female migrant from Poland, small town). Besides, such cultural knowledge of how to communicate is not about the language itself, but also about how to behave in different cultures.
>
> (male migrant from Poland, from middle town, born in 1989)

In addition to language, migrants also learn non-verbal intercultural communication. This is primarily a question of, simply put, being kind towards other people. Non-verbal communication is also associated with nuanced racism (Gawlewicz, 2015), especially if migrants themselves experienced discriminatory behaviour due to their ethnicity.

> (…) and the experience of communing with other cultures in general, it is interesting. So there are two things I guess. It depends on the person, how open one is, how tolerant one is, because one either brings the bad, the negative or the positive things, it depends on what and who one meets.
>
> (male migrant from Poland, from middle town, born in 1988)

In describing the effects of their experience abroad, a number of interviewed migrants specifically referred to soft skills, even using those exact words:

> I think soft skills. Such a broad understanding of certain aspects and various perspectives, that everyone is a different person, which is why I am now looking for a way to get along with someone. I know that everyone can be brought up in different cultures, families, and it is of great importance (…) not being so closed in the bubble in which you grew up. And I think that you gain such a greater openness, like a broader perspective.
>
> (female migrant from middle town in Poland, born in 1990)

In their early study of Slovakian migrants, Williams and Baláž (2005) argue that language can be a source of skill acquisition for various soft skills, such as self-confidence, networking skills, learning to adapt and self-reliance. Their study showed that, for Slovak *au pairs* in the UK, learning and knowledge creation could take place not only in the workplace, but also within the private sphere of a home (cf. Williams, 2007: 374).

Having experienced international migration helps people develop flexibility and adaptability to changes, especially changes of employer, sector or job content. This may lead to job-hopping, i.e. frequent job changes, or labour market flexibility (Grugulis and Vincent, 2009).

When working abroad, most migrants show discipline, commitment and punctuality (Lafer, 2004), which are qualities appreciated by employers. For many employers who recruit migrants for simple, routine jobs, the main reason to do so is their attitude to work. In many host countries, migration gives opportunities for employers to hire people they can count on and who perform their tasks well. While it is of course true that people usually migrate for financial reasons, money can never replace the strong emotional need for being appreciated by other people.

During migration, people also learn autonomy-control, especially in the workplace, where there are clearly defined boundaries and responsibilities, as well as (often if not always) unwritten rules of organizational culture (Hampson and Junor, 2010). This favours the practice of capacity for reflexivity (Archer, 2007). The practice of reflexivity starts when during migration, in social situations people experience the moments of surprise, so called "aha moments" (Grabowska, 2018).

The ability to work autonomously is also connected with employee maturity, life experience and the ability to deal with failures. While migration experience and encounters with other people do not necessarily yield immediate effects that translate into professional career achievements. Soft skills acquired and strengthened during migration may yield results in one's career in a slightly later period.

Another skill that many migrants learn is how to deal with stress; in other words, stress resilience. They come to understand that the workplace is not necessarily a source of discomfort and tension, and that it can be a source of satisfaction.

> I have such a nice example, because what I learned in my work was the English language and what England taught me. It taught me less stress at work. We have something like this, we Poles have been practically raised since childhood with stress (...) And here I struggled for a long time with learning not to stress.
>
> (female migrant from Poland, middle town, migrant in the UK)

As a result of their experiences, international migrants increase their self-efficacy, which may affect their behaviour and actions in various spheres of life.

> I became independent. I can do a lot of things myself. In the UK I was practically on my own. The English I knew from my education was not enough, it was different from what was really spoken. Phone calls were a problem, for example. I was shaking like jelly on a plate when I needed to make a phone call. I could not. I always asked someone to do it for me in the office. Now it is ok. I'm so brave. I don't need anyone to support me to do something more formal like this. Because I did not feel like going in a suit and signing a contract for a million dollars. Now I think I would be able to do it. I am also so more open to people.
>
> (female migrant from a middle town in Poland, born 1991)

> Migration sheds all your complexes if you are disabled. It gives you strength and perseverance. You know that you can do things that you would not even think about in Poland.
>
> (female migrant from Poland, born 1988)

The capacity to cope with "emotion work" (Hochschild, 1979) constitutes another important part of MigCap (Grabowska, 2018). It is an important factor in an individual's commitment to their work, the ability to control their emotions, persistence and creativity in carrying out tasks, as well as the ability to cope with boredom, especially during extended periods of manual and routine work. Coping with emotional work also affects the building and maintaining of relationships with colleagues and superiors and the coordination of work performed by others (Hampson and Junor, 2010).

By working abroad in the services industry, migrants acquire universal skills in customer interaction and service. This may not appear to be a unique skill, but during migration, migrants learn a broader skill: the ability to perform emotional work (Hochschild, 1979). These skills are also related to Psychological Capital: controlling one's emotions, non-aggressive communication, self-awareness and awareness of others, how to behave in specific situations and solving situational problems (Hampson and Junor, 2010). The acquisition of services skills is conducive to exercising reflexivity.

> I think that working in services, sales [abroad], with the client, gives a human an ability to listen and understand the client. These are very valuable experiences. (…) I know from my boss that when I started working in Poland (…) these were very important experiences transferred from abroad, despite the fact that the work was in the real estate consulting sector.
>
> (female migrant from Poland, born in 1990)

Service industry skills are soft skills: they relate to work in a relational and emotional environment. Service workers must constantly monitor their surroundings and ensure that customers are comfortable. The fact that this type of soft skill is not much appreciated by employers, especially where returning migrants are concerned, has to do with the lack of formal certification for these skills. This is why written recommendations from employers are so important in this industry. These soft skills can also be classified as tacit skills (Evans, Kersh and Kontiainen, 2004): skills obtained in jobs that do not themselves require specific qualifications, but can pay off later on in one's career.

Box 5.1 Testimonials from Slovakia

Stefan

> "I understand CNN and the BBC and am more self-confident"; for him, these television channels were icons of access to broader spheres of (different) knowledge.
>
> Williams and Baláž (2005: 459)

Peter

> I became an entrepreneur after my return from the UK. I needed English to communicate with clients, some of whom are foreign. I speak good English now, which is essential for that. I think my social status also improved because I learned English.
>
> Williams and Baláž (2005: 462)

Zdeno

> English was essential for my career...
>
> Williams and Baláž (2005: 462)

Peter

> The most valuable thing I obtained in the UK was a total change in my frame of mind. I became self-confident and learned the English way of "taking it easy" when dealing with problems.
>
> Williams and Baláž (2005: 459)

Robert

> "The most valuable experience I obtained in the UK was not so much professional skills - I could learn these anywhere - as the ability to manage crises and to communicate."
>
> Williams and Baláž (2005: 459)

Box 5.2 Vignette: A nurse from a small town in Western Poland, and her communication skills

A nurse from a small town in Poland experienced social learning in the workplace in the UK. She spoke English with the residents of a nursing home from the war and post-war generations. She learned to speak English as it was spoken during the beginning and middle of the 20th century, which differed from contemporary English. It was noticeable, for example when she went to the pub with her colleagues. She experienced a difference of contexts not only between the sending and receiving countries, but also within the receiving country itself.

> Well, at the beginning it was actually the residents [of the nursery home] who taught me English. They were ladies aged 80–90–100 who remembered Poles through the prism of WW2, aviation and when they learnt I am Polish, they treated me with great respect, sympathy and openness to talk. That is why I learned the language quickly, because my patients mobilized me, told me to read the newspaper, read books, so that I would learn quickly. They spoke a language like this .. it was mother English, such as Old Polish, such an unused language, such old fashion. And I learned to speak such a language from these patients and when I went to the pub with the English folks, when I spoke, they cried with laughter, because no one had such expressions anymore … I spoke this language really in Old English (…) yes, yes, they taught me so that I could speak English jargon … Well, it was impressive, the ladies taught me to speak like that. I thought that everyone would say so (…) Because then I found out what farmer's language is. I also learned a little this way, to be understandable, to speak like them and to emphasize a bit too … But I spoke to my patients the way the old ladies taught me. And very much … They always corrected me. When I was leaving, the patients made a contribution them- selves, because they collected money to say a good-bye to me and farewell cards – I had good contact, very good.
>
> (female migrant from a small Polish town, born in 1980)

To summarise, the acquisition of mind and soft components of MigCap involves both the individual and the relational dimension. In the individual dimension, it concerns becoming familiar with and learning to understand the environment in which the migrant absorbs the social world (or fails to). They may do this instrumentally, selectively, routinely and perhaps reflexively, reflecting on themselves and their position in this new, differ- ent social context. In the relational dimension, MigCap acquisition has to do with interaction with other, often culturally different people. The acquisition is related to the establishment and maintaining of relationships in social spaces. These interactions and the resultant social relationships can be enriching, even if they involve the effort of communicating with and getting to know other people. It is important to open up to the other person, without any initial judgment. An instrumental approach, oriented for example only at earning money, may cause discouragement in contacts, and in extreme cases lead to xenophobic behaviour and, as a result, to the inability to build social relations on which cooperation is based. This obstructs the acquisition and development of informal human capital.

In the relational dimension, the impact of migration on informal human capital is related to the establishment of interpersonal contacts and the building and maintaining of social relations in diverse socio-cultural contexts.

Soft and maker skills

The acquisition of linguistic and cognitive skills strengthens communicative skills in general, which in turn facilitates the acquisition of further components of informal human capital that involve cooperation and teamwork.

> [I have learned] to work with people, work in a team. It is very important. I have no problems with it. I also gained such courage with communication, certainly in talking to foreign-speaking people, that I do not have this problem, because in gastronomy it is known that it often happens that someone comes from abroad and you need to talk to this person, I don't feel this anymore. Such a border, it is known that, as I said before, this language is not at a fantastic level, but I do not feel such a barrier anymore, where many people have such a barrier.
>
> (female migrant from a small town in Poland, born in 1988)

Acquiring teamwork skills helps migrants improve their work productivity, develop a goal-oriented attitude, learn to adapt to changes, increase their morale and motivation, and establish cordial relationships. A large part of teamwork has to do with achieving synergy in complex work processes. It therefore helps to understand the complexity of work and to improve one's relevant soft skills.

For Mexicans migrants, especially men, teamwork skills often go hand in hand with "maker" skills. This is because they usually learn through practice in cooperation with others in a team.

Box 5.3 Small picture from Mexico: Teamwork combined with maker skills

Omar, a 40-year-old immigrant and skilled stone mason from Mexico City, described team-based training methods that he learned starting

at the age of 14 when he first entered Mexico City's high-end resi-
dential construction market. Omar was part of an informal team made
up of half a dozen workers with a range of construction skills and
experiences, particularly in stone and brick masonry. He initially
secured access to the team through an uncle, also a skilled mason in
Mexico City. As he put it, the team method helped to broaden the
knowledge base of the entire team and allowed them to cope with
unforeseen building challenges and bottlenecks. Additionally, his
uncle and other family members helped to supplement team-based
learning through informal individual mentoring. Under this supervision
Omar developed a range of skills in masonry and stonework and
related tasks, such as concrete pouring and finishing. In North Carolina Omar, now as a high-ranking field supervisor and occasional
independent contractor, reproduces many of these same practices
by providing structured training to immigrant friends. Interestingly, he
is not always compensated for this training support, which often
takes place in less-formal work settings.

Lowe, Hagan and Iskander (2010: 217)

Migrants appreciate the acquisition of manual, technical skills, next to
the soft skills, especially if they had a structure of opportunities in the
workplace to acquire them.

> I also acquired everything there, but I value the skills that I have
> acquired the most, such as interpersonal relations. Apart from such
> technical things, because I am a cook, I graduated from a cooking
> school, I made a master chef there and it is not as important as the
> ability to interact with different people. Because I lived, I shared a
> kitchen with a person from Sri Lanka, Ecuador, Romania, Germany, and
> Italy, and these were very close contacts and I had to learn to talk and
> communicate with everyone, and that is what I appreciate the most.
>
> (male migrant from Poland, small town, born in 1986)

By experiencing work abroad, in different places of employment, in various positions and in various sectors, people can learn to understand it as a
process, see its meaning (e.g. during meetings, so-called morning briefings).
Migrants talk about acquiring the skill to coordinate tasks at a given time.

It is worth taking a moment to specifically examine the soft skills
relating to the intrapersonal dimension: the ability to cope with boredom,

to engage in monotonous, repetitive, routine and usually manual tasks (Hampson and Junor, 2010). Skills related to coping with boredom build the perseverance that the modern labour market requires.

> When cleaning pub toilets, I realized how difficult these dirty and simple jobs are. I respect all the people who do this. I was doing this job as best I could. I learned patience. While cleaning the toilets, I started to think about what to do with myself, how to continue my education.
> (from the biographical narrative of Matilda from Poland, a graduate of social sciences, born in 1988)

For people with high cultural capital, having performed routine tasks at some stage in their professional career may contribute to autonomous reflexivity (Grabowska, 2018).

Summary

The analysis of limited data regarding Mexicans and Central Europeans conducted in this chapter revealed that MigCap acquisition occurs in both of these ethnic groups, even though they are sociodemographic different, as the analysis of their profiles in Chapter 4 attests. We identified richer data relating the acquisition of MigCap linked to Central Europeans than to Mexicans.

The various data sources presented in this chapter also showed that the acquisition of MigCap requires human agency and a favourable, relational environment in which people can observe, communicate and cooperate with others, in teams.

One of the key findings across all ethnic groups under study, supported by quantitative data, is the exceptionally high value that migrants place on the development of communication skills. As the discussion showed, the acquisition of English as a language resource/capital was highly ranked by all migrant groups under study. In particular, we emphasised that the acquisition of English language skill is not only a mind skill, but also a soft skill, as it facilitates listening, communicating, learning and negotiating.

This chapter also addressed the obstruction of MigCap acquisition. We were able to conduct this analysis based on the Polish case only. Migrants who did not acquire MigCap were mostly men who were abroad for less than a year. In most cases, these individuals engaged primarily in seasonal migration and were focused only on earning, not learning and earning.

Particular attention was also devoted to the acquisition of teamwork skills in combination with communication and maker skills. According to our findings, teamwork skills combined with maker skills are best developed, mobilised and therefore acquired in relational social spaces where people can talk and do things together.

Another soft skill acquired through international migration that we were able to identify was flexibility. In the 21st century, flexibility promotes adjustability and enhances resilience.

We were also able to show that the skills for emotional work can be developed through international migration, especially in the service sector, where migrants usually work, and they can learn through observation, communication and hands-on experience.

The distinction between and separation of the acquisition of MigCap from the transfer thereof that has been established in this book helps us analyse the process of flowing MigCap. We were able to distinguish what and how humans acquire MigCap from what people do with these new resources as regards, among other things, their position in the labour market, social mobility, teamwork, productivity, contributions to organisational culture and well-being. These "ends or end products" will be analysed, interpreted and discussed in detail in the following chapter devoted to transfer of MigCap.

References

Archer, M. S. (2007). *Making our way through the world: Human reflexivity and social mobility*. Cambridge University Press.

Archer, M. S. (2015). Socialization as relational reflexivity. In P. Donati and M.S. Archer (eds.), *Relational Subject* (123–154). Cambridge: Cambridge University Press.

Arrow, K. (1962). The Economic Implications of Learning by Doing. *Review of Economic Studies*, 29, 155–174.

Baláž, V., Williams, A. M., Moravčíková, K., and Chrančoková, M. (2019). What competences, which migrants? Tacit and explicit knowledge acquired via migration. *Journal of Ethnic and Migration Studies*, 47(8), 1758–1774.

Baláž, V. and Williams, A. M. (2004). 'Been there, done that': international student migration and human capital transfers from the UK to Slovakia. *Population, space and place*, 10(3), 217–237.

Baláž, V., Williams, A. M., and Kollar, D. (2004). Temporary versus permanent youth brain drain: economic implications. *International Migration*, 42(4), 3–34.

Donati, P. and Archer, M. S. (2015). *The relational subject*. Cambridge: Cambridge University Press.

Dustmann, C. (1999). Temporary migration, human capital, and language fluency of migrants. *Scandinavian Journal of Economics*, 101(2), 297–314.

Evans, K., Kersh, N., and Kontiainen, S. (2004). Recognition of tacit skills: sustaining learning outcomes in adult learning and work re-entry. *International Journal of Training and Development*, 8(1), 54–72.

Garapich, M. P. (2014). Homo sovieticus revisited–anti-institutionalism, alcohol and resistance among Polish homeless men in London. *International Migration*, 52(1), 100–117.

Gawlewicz, A. (2015). Beyond 'us' and 'them': migrant encounters with difference and redefining the national. *Fennia*, 193(2), 198–211.

Grabowska, I. (2018). Social skills, workplaces and social remittances: a case of post-accession migrants. *Work, Employment and Society*, 32(5), 868–886.

Grabowska, I. and Jastrzebowska, A. (2019). The impact of migration on human capacities of two generations of Poles: The interplay of the individual and the social in human capital approaches. *Journal of Ethnic and Migration Studies*, 47 (8), 1829–1847.

Grabowska, I. and Jastrzebowska, A. (under review). *Migrant Informal Human Capital of Returnees*.

Green, F. (2011). *What is Skill?: An Interdisciplinary Synthesis*. London: Centre for Learning and Life Chances in Knowledge Economies and Societies.

Grugulis, I. and Vincent, S. (2009). Whose skill is it anyway? 'soft' skills and polarization. Work. *Employment and Society*, 23(4), 597–615.

Habermas, J. (1992). *Autonomy and solidarity: interviews with Jürgen Habermas*. New York: Verso.

Hagan, J., Demonsant, J. L., and Chávez, S. (2014). Identifying and measuring the lifelong human capital of "Unskilled" migrants in the Mexico-US migratory circuit. *Journal on migration and Human Security*, 2(2), 76–100.

Hagan, J., Hernández-León, R., and Demonsant, J. L. (2015). *Skills of the unskilled: Work and mobility among Mexican migrants*. Oakland: University of California Press.

Hampson, I. and Junor, A. (2010). Putting the process back in: Rethinking service sector skill. *Work, Employment and Society*, 24(3), 526–545.

Haynes, M. and Galasińska, A. (2016). Narrating migrant workplace experiences: Social remittances to Poland as knowledge of British workplace cultures. *Central and Eastern European Migration Review*, 5(2), 41–62.

Hochschild, A. R. (1979). Emotion work, feeling rules, and social structure. *American Journal of Sociology*, 85(3), 551–575.

Janta, H., Jephcote, C., Williams, A. M., and Li, G. (2019). Returned migrants acquisition of competences: the contingencies of space and time. *Journal of Ethnic and Migration Studies*, 47(8), 1740–1757.

Jarvis, P. (2007). *Globalization, lifelong learning and the learning society: Sociological perspectives*. Oxfordshire: Routledge.

Lafer, G. (2004). What is 'skill'? Training for discipline in the low-wage labour market. *The skills that matter*, London: Palgrave.

Levitt, P. (1998). Social remittances: Migration driven local-level forms of cultural diffusion. *International Migration Review*, 32(4), 926–948.

Levitt, P. (2001). *The transnational villagers*. Berkeley: University of California Press.

Lowe, N., Hagan, J.M., and Iskander. N. (2010). Revealing Talent: Informal Skills Intermediation as an Emergent Pathway to Immigrant Labor Market Incorporation. *Environment and Planning A: Economy and Space*, 42(1): 205–222.

Lundvall, B. Ä. and Johnson, B. (1994). The learning economy. *Journal of Industry Studies*, 1(2), 23–42.

Marsick, V. J. and Watkins, K. E. (2001). Informal and incidental learning. *New directions for adult and continuing education*, 89, 25.

Monteith, W. and Giesbert, L. (2017). 'When the stomach is full we look for respect': perceptions of 'good work' in the urban informal sectors of three developing countries. *Work, Employment and Society*, 31(5), 816–833.

Moroşanu, L., King, R., Lulle, A., and Pratsinakis, M. (2019). 'One improves here every day': the occupational and learning journeys of 'lower-skilled' European migrants in the London region. *Journal of Ethnic and Migration Studies*, 47(8), 1775–1792.

Polanyi, M. (2009). *The tacit dimension*. Chicago: University of Chicago Press.

Shan, H. (2013). Skill as a relational construct: hiring practices from the standpoint of Chinese immigrant engineers in Canada. *Work, Employment and Society*, 27 (6), 915–931.

Thomas, W. I. and Znaniecki, F. (1996). *The Polish peasant in Europe and America: A classic work in immigration history*. Champaign Illinois: University of Illinois Press.

Wenger, E. (1998). Communities of practice: Learning as a social system. *Systems Thinker*, 9(5), 2–3.

Williams, A. M. (2007). Listen to me, learn with me: International migration and knowledge transfer. *British journal of industrial relations*, 45(2), 361–382.

Williams, A. M. (2009). Employability and international migration: theoretical perspectives. In S. MacKay (ed.), *Refugees, Recent Migrants and Employment, challenging barriers and exploring pathways* (23–34). Oxford: Routledge.

Williams, A. M. and Baláž, V. (2005). What Human Capital, Which Migrants? Returned Skilled Migration to Slovakia From the UK. *International Migration Review*, 39(2), 439–468.

6 Migratory transfer of informal human capital

Introduction

When someone returns home from abroad, family members usually ask: what did you bring? The returnee opens his or her suitcase and takes out gifts, souvenirs, postcards, photos, etc. Unfortunately, one cannot similarly produce from one's suitcase intangible migration acquisitions related to informal human capital: mind skills, soft skills, maker skills and life skills.

"Transfer" in this book does not refer to social transfers between countries in the form of welfare benefits. It does not refer to the transfer of migration money – economic remittances – between receiving and sending countries, between companies, households, or individuals. In this book, the concept of "transfer" has a socio-cultural meaning and is closest to the psychological understanding of the transfer of skills, competences, attitudes and behaviours acquired as learning outcomes. In the literature "transfer" also refers to the distribution of resources in the mental, social and cultural dimensions (Hodkinson and Hodkinson, 2004). In this book, migratory transfer is linked to the transfer of informal human capital, MigCap. What we discuss is the phenomenon of transfer between areas of human activity in geographical space. As Williams and Baláž (2008b) claim, migration is the channel for learning and knowledge transfer. It puts skills, competences and knowledge into motion which otherwise would be immovable.

This chapter addresses the following research questions: what is transferred, how it is transferred, from where (country of migration), to where (country of origin) and by whom. The inquiries into these questions will be based on both quantitative data (big picture) and qualitative data (meso and micro perspectives).

Acquiring skills is part of the learning process. Learning through experience, which takes place during the human experience of new situations, including in migratory contexts, is a continuous activity of acquiring new knowledge (Kolb, 2000).

DOI: 10.4324/9781003011545-6

In order to use the knowledge one has acquired and to transfer it to another sphere of life. It is necessary to have motivation to act and a high level of social competence to be able to use the acquired knowledge in life. The ability to transfer skills enables personal development and full participation in professional and social life and, consequently, work and life satisfaction (Kanchier, 2000; Naimark and Pearce, 1985).

To compare and contrast the two processes: the acquisition of a resource is the reception of information by a person from their environment, while transfer is the transmission of a resource from a person to their environment (see Figure 6.1.).

In migration studies, the transfer of human capital is usually interpreted as "brain drain" or "brain waste", which is associated with the transfer of high-quality human capital from less developed countries to more developed countries. There is also a "brain exchange", which assumes a more balanced form of human capital flow from places where there is a surplus of human capital to areas where there is a lack of people with certain qualifications. Another related concept is "brain training", which is linked to strengthening human capital through learning and training. The concept that defines migration-related human capital transfers is "brain circulation", in which human capital is strengthened through temporary foreign mobility experiences (cf. Williams and Baláž, 2005, 2008a).

On the one hand, the simplest, analytically tangible and best-known indicator of the transfer of human capital in international spaces is the recognition of diplomas and degrees from various types of schools, which go hand in hand with knowledge of the language of the host country, so that the acquired formal qualifications can be used in the new professional environment.

On the other hand, the researchers emphasise that the transfer of skills acquired during migration can occur not only with people doing jobs that require high qualifications, but also with people doing work that requires no qualifications at all (cf. Hagan et al., 2015). Researchers claim that migrants are dichotomously classified into skilled and unskilled too easily, and that there are in fact many more categories (Williams and Baláž, 2005,

Figure 6.1 Visualisation of skill transfer as a result of skill acquisition
Source: Author's elaboration.

2008a; see also: Hagan et al., 2015; Grabowska, Jaźwińska, 2015; Grabowska, 2016, 2018).

Sen's capability approach, to which we referred in the second chapter of this book, changes the focus from means – i.e. the resources people have – to ends – i.e. what they are able to do with these resources. This shift in focus is justified because having resources and goods alone does not ensure that people will be able to convert them into actual actions. Two people with similar sets of goods and resources may achieve very different ends depending on their circumstances.[1]

This chapter discusses these ends: what are people able to do with their informal human capital acquired or enhanced through international migration.

Macro perspective

The availability of quantitative data regarding the scale, nature and location of MigCap transfer is not equal for the countries studied in this book: Mexico and various countries of Central Europe.

For Mexico, the results of the research by Hagan et al. (2015) on migration between Mexico and the US, published in the monograph with the meaningful title *Skills of the Unskilled*, show the transfer of competences in the transnational space. The authors emphasise that the transfer of competences should be studied in both directions, i.e. as a circulation between the sending and receiving country, and that it should be studied in the course of life. It is also crucial to determine who can transfer competences, in what institutional and structural conditions is able to mobilise them in order to improve their social and professional situation after their return. The study by Hagan et al. (2015) found that the acquisition itself and the strengthening of the competences does not guarantee transfer.

Hagan et al. (2015) also found that one in five migrants had transferred social competences from the USA back to Mexico (17 percent of men and 32 percent of women), while in the other direction, from Mexico to the US, this was only 3 percent (2 percent men and 4 percent women). This means that the transfer of social competences is spatially and sexually conditioned. More men than women (40 percent to 32 percent) transferred technical skills acquired in the workplace. Because they more often perform so-called emotion work (Hochschild, 1979) in the service, care and housework sectors, women were less likely than men working in construction and agriculture to acquire and strengthen social competences as a result of migration. Another reason why women strengthened their MigCap more than men is because the social spaces in which they stayed offered greater opportunities to practice linguistic and communicative competences in general.

Table 6.1 Transfer of skills by Mexican migrants (percent)

	From Mexico to United States			From United States to Mexico		
	Total N=200	Men n=172	Women n=25	Total n=200	Men n=172	Women n=25
Any transfer	48	51	26	51	50	56
English	2	1	4	11	10	18
Formal education	1	1	0	2	2	0
On-the-job technical skills	44	47	26	30	40	32
Off-the-job-technical skills	11	12	4	0	0	0
Social skills	3	2	4	19	17	32

Source: cf. Hagan et al. (2015: 161, Table 5.2).

Hagan et al. (2015) also showed that migrants are aware that employers appreciate the social competences of employees, but are not willing to pay more for them. This may cause return migrants to look for a place in the labour market where they want to be located and cause so-called job-hopping or temporary withdrawal from the market, e.g. to receive unemployment benefits (cf. Iglicka, 2009 in her research on post-accession migrants).

The research findings of Hagan, Demonsant and Chávez (2014: 93) suggest that manual, maker skills are not the only skills that promote the development of entrepreneurial activities in local economies. Also very important are the language and social skills that returnees bring back with them. Fifty-four percent of the *patrones*[2] and 76 percent of self-employed return migrants acquired such skills in the US and were able to utilise them in their business ventures. Around 35 percent reported transferring English language skills to their entrepreneurial activities.

Soft skills acquired during international migration that escape the standard ways in which human capital is measured can include punctuality, the ability to work and cooperate in groups; supervisory and leadership skills; entrepreneurial attitudes, especially with regard to taking initiative; self-confidence; and personal skills that support personal development. Hagan et al. (2015) found that for unqualified jobs, employers "recruit" an approach, attitude and commitment to work linked to punctuality and following instructions.

Hagan et al. (2015) also note that working abroad helps improve migrants' opportunities for social and economic mobility upon return (see Tables 6.2. and 6.3.). This depends on the informal skills that migrants are

Table 6.2 Indicators of social mobility across the migratory circuit of Mexicans (in per cent)

	Before Migrating		In the US		On Return	
	Men n=168	Women n=22	Men n=171	Women n=28	Men n=161	Women n=20
Satisfied with a job	69	78	84	89	73	76
Transitioned to a higher skill job*	32	27	39	27	29	44
Mean skill level**	1.8	1.5	1.8	1.4	2.1	1.6

*Among those who had more than one job at any given stage
**1: low-skilled; 2: semi-skilled; 3: high-skilled.
Source: Hagan, Demonsant and Chávez (2014).

Table 6.3 Indicators of economic mobility in US labour market (in per cent), $N=200$

Learned new skills, reskilling in US	81*
Transited to a better job requiring more skills	36
Wage increase	33
Skills recognised and rewarded	65**

*68 per cent learned new skills through on-the-job observation and 56 per cent through explicit instruction
from my boss or co-worker.
** Of these, 52 percent received a raise; 12 percent were asked to teach others a skill; 19 percent reported receiving more autonomy at work; and 17 percent were given more responsibility on the job.
Source: cf. Hagan, Demonsant and Chávez (2014: 88: Table 7).

able to transfer. Beneficial skills in this context especially concern attitude to work, the ability to learn socially (being open-minded), previous experience working with people.

For Central Europe, particularly for Poland, Tomescu-Dubrow (2015) found that migration experiences of two months or more involving working and living abroad increased migrants' tacit knowledge. Such knowledge is beneficial in that it increases one's attractiveness to employers, independently of other important resources, also linked to formal education. This translates in particular into the level of human capital, including competencies, net income and entrepreneurial ability, which can be understood as business knowledge, recognition of market needs and investment opportunities, the ability to reduce one's personal or business expenses in order to have more money left over. The effect of migration enhancement in the POLPAN data[3] for Poland is particularly visible among people who had already demonstrated entrepreneurial ability as self-employed persons while Poland was still a communist economy. It is true that the POLPAN data does not provide any answers as to why people return to Poland, but Tomescu-Dubrow presumes that returning migrants see opportunities in their home country, especially with regard to starting up a business. Experience working abroad can offer greater benefits when migrants' return is motivated by opportunities, and not forced by circumstances beyond their control. Regardless of the reasons behind the return of the migrants participating in the POLPAN survey, the analysis demonstrated that working and living abroad had a positive impact on the tacit human capital and labour market success.

Based on quantitative data from the Strategic Consulting Centre (CDS) (Szymańska, Ulasiński and Bieńkowska, 2012) obtained through surveys among households in three large regions in Poland (Malopolska, Silesia and Lower Silesia), it was found out which non-material resources returning migrants brought with them. This included basic skills, such as was improved communication in a foreign language (Lower Silesia: 60 percent, Silesia: 90 percent, Malopolska: 38 percent) and migration contacts (Lower Silesia: 83 percent, Silesia: 80 percent, Malopolska: 82 percent). Moreover, migrants declared that they had gained more confidence in themselves and in their own abilities (Lower Silesia: 80 percent, Silesia: 83 percent, Malopolska: 73 percent).

In the CDS survey conducted around 2009, respondents from the selected regions were asked to indicate which kinds of tacit knowledge they had obtained through migration and subsequently put to use in Poland. The results were: an entrepreneurial attitude (Lower Silesia: 12 percent, Silesia: 23 percent); ability to install technological solutions (Lower Silesia: 58 percent, Malopolska: 42 percent, Silesia: 64 percent), organisational and management skills (Lower Silesia: 68 percent, Silesia: 62 percent); and qualifications acquired as a result of vocational training during migration (Lower Silesia: 68 percent, Malopolska: 45 percent, Silesia: 31 percent).

Based on the data derived from the most recent comparative survey of Polish and Lithuanian returnees, which was conducted in 2020 (the DAINA CEEYouth research project), we were able to create a Migration Skill Transfer Index (see Table 6.4 and Table 6.5). To create this index, we summarised the six categories of skills used in the question: what skills acquired in the UK do you use after returning? The respondents could choose from the following options: teamwork, leadership skills, knowledge of English, stress resistance, entrepreneurship and taking initiative.

The Migration Skill Transfer Index ranges from 0 to 6, where 0 means that a person has not transferred any of the skills listed in the survey, and 6 means

Table 6.4 Transfer of skills acquired abroad by Polish and Lithuanian returnees

	Poland		Lithuania	
	n	%	n	%
Knowledge of English	212	41.1	93	45.1
Teamwork	170	32.9	80	38.8
Stress resistance	173	33.5	70	34.0
Taking the initiative	122	23.6	73	35.4
Leadership skills	77	14.9	51	24.8
Entrepreneurship	88	17.1	28	13.6

Source: DAINA CEEYouth research project.

that a person has transferred all of them. Nearly 60 percent of people declared that they transferred at least one of the six mind and soft skills mentioned. In the group of Polish returnees, nearly 40 percent of people did not transfer any mind and soft skills; 44 percent of Lithuanian returnees did not transfer any informal skills.

Table 6.5 Migration Skill Transfer Index of returnees to Poland and Lithuania

	PL		LT	
	n	%	n	%
0	205	39.7	90	43.7
1	88	17.1	14	6.8
2	68	13.2	23	11.2
3	65	12.6	23	11.2
4	49	9.5	28	13.6
5	19	3.7	14	6.8
6	22	4.3	14	6.8
M	1.63		1.92	
Me	1.00		1.00	
Mo	0.00		0.00	
SD	1.77		2.05	
Min	0.00		0.00	
Max	6.00		6.00	

The comparative Polish-Lithuanian survey with return migrants conducted in May–July 2020 within the DAINA CEEYouth; total PL n=516; LT n=206; only completed questionnaires.
Source: Author's elaboration.

The transfer of mind and soft skills was less common among Polish migrants ($M=1.63$; $SD=1.77$) than among Lithuanian migrants ($M=1.91$; $SD=2.05$). The difference is significant at the level of the statistical trend t $(344.72)=1.758$, $p=0.080$.

Using regression analysis, we investigated on the basis of which factors described from the perspective of the domains of life (work, education, housing, relations), it was possible to predict the values in the Migration Skill Transfer Index.

We found that 33 percent of the Migration Skill Transfer Index variability can be predicted on the basis of work, education, housing and relations. The transfer of MigCap is more beneficial for people who are employed ($B=1.555$; $p<0.001$), are in a relationship ($B=1.993$; $p<0.01$), have higher education ($B=0.473$; $p<0.001$), do not live alone ($B=-0.868$; $p<0.05$) and were abroad for a period of five to 10 years. This regression

Table 6.6 Multiple linear regression with Migration Skill Transfer Index for Polish and Lithuanian returnees

	MIGRATION SKILL TRANSFER INDEX	
	B	SE
Constant		
Sex (ref=men) women	0.309	0.501
Domain 1. Education (ref=other than higher) higher	0.473***	0.123
Domain 2. Labour market situation (ref=unemployed) inactive employed	-0.398 1.555***	0.308 0.279
Domain 3. Housing (ref=own) rent with someone	-0.658 -0.868*	0.390 0.389
Domain 4. Relations (ref=no) yes	1.993**	0.638
Back to the same place (ref=yes) no	0.228	0.212
Time of migration (ref=1–5) 5–10 years More than 10	0.349* 0.209	0.141 0.145
Adjusted R^2	0.328	

*** $p<0.001$; ** $p<0.01$; * $p<0.05$.

Source: Author's elaboration; the comparative Polish-Lithuanian survey with return migrants conducted in May-July 2020 within the DAINA CEEYouth; total PL n=516; LT n=206; only completed questionnaires.

analysis tells us that there is a *Matthew Effect*[4] in the transferral of MigCap: the better the educational and labour market situation of an individual, the more informal human capital migration allows them to transfer. Also, in order to make the transfer of MigCap possible, it is important to have a continuous migratory history of more than five years. In other words the time is needed abroad to acquire MigCap as a resource for transfer internationally.

Selectivity of MigCap acquisition and transfer

Migration studies explore selectivity and prove that migrants do not select randomly from the home country's population and enquire: "(…) how, from a pool of potential migrants, do the particular individuals and families who actually migrate select themselves or become selected? Societal structures, individual human capital, family economies, and social capital set parameters" (Harzig, Hoerder and Gabaccia, 2009: 91).

> (…) socio-demographic selectivity is also useful for surmising some of the root causes and potential consequences of migration for sending and receiving areas and for investigating them further. Given the paucity of detailed data for many immigrant groups, socio-demographic profiles of both emigrants and return migrants have helped scholars to understand migration trends, particularly at the regional and global levels.
>
> (Lutz, Butz and KC, 2014: 348)

"Demographic characteristics can also be useful for the indirect estimations and forecasting of migration, given that many migration flows exhibit relatively stable demographic patterns" (Lutz, Butz, and KC, 2014: 348).

Economics of migration is primarily concerned with the nature (positive, negative and neutral), causes and effects of the (self-)*selection of migrants* (Biavaschi and Elsner, 2013). When skilled migrants leave their home country, we talk about positive selection, because migration poses a hurdle for the low-skilled (Chiswick, 1999). When low-skilled migrants leave their home country, we speak of negative selection (Borjas, 1987). When migrants display the same skill, on average, as those left behind, we talk about natural selection. The situation becomes more complicated when studying return and temporary migrants. Borjas (1985) argues that return migration is partially biased because only the most successful remain, and if a whole cohort remains, assimilation rates are lower. Temporary migrants do not select intuitively to relieve constraints in the local labour markets – many people who perform well locally choose to migrate.

Thus far, migration selectivity has not been studied in relation to the destination countries from which various components of informal human capital are transferred. In fact, only one Polish database allows for the analysis of the selectivity of informal human capital transfer, and this is only possible thanks to the very large research sample it offers: approximately 4,000 migrants. In this data, it is possible to distinguish people who returned to Poland from Germany, the Netherlands and the British Isles, which also provides the opportunity to look at other linguistic contexts, in addition to English. Among Mexicans, Slovaks and Lithuanians, migration is primarily to and from English-speaking countries, preventing the performance of any selectivity analysis linked to destination countries where other languages than English are spoken.

It is clear from our selectivity analysis (Table 6.7) that when differentiate based on migration destination country and various properties of formal and informal human capital, there are important differences to be found (cf. Grabowska and Jastrzebowska, forthcoming).

Compared to migrants from Poland who worked in the Netherlands and the British Isles, migrants who worked in Germany were predominately employed (67.8 percent). The employed group consisted mostly of people born between 1968 and 1982 (56.5 percent). This cohort earned the lowest wage (M=2473.88 PLN), but was also most likely to set up their own businesses (15.9 percent). The employed group had the highest job satisfaction (M=3.71), but scored lowest on well-being (M=1.37) and individual soft skills (M=3.35). Migrants who had worked in Germany also had the highest level of formal human capital and the lowest informal capital. There are various possible explanations for this. First, many well-educated Polish people (e.g. teachers, nurses, municipal clerks) engage in seasonal jobs in Germany's agricultural sector. Second, due to the fact that they worked seasonally and in a pendulum way (e.g. nine months in Poland and two or three months in Germany), without embedding into the German labour market, they did not acquire and/or enhance soft skills. Thirdly, the German labour market is oriented towards the recognition of formal education and vocational training.

We found the highest levels of well-being among migrants who had worked in the Netherlands (M=1.45), although they also displayed the lowest job satisfaction (M=3.57), despite the fact that they earned the highest wage after return (M=2737.55 PLN). This high level of well-being might have to do with observing and learning from Dutch employees, who are very effective and draw a clear line between working time and leisure time. Migrants to the Netherlands were younger than migrants to Germany and the British Isles. Migrants who did temporary work in the British Isles were the best-educated group (M=12.53 years of education), which is in line with the findings of Kaczmarczyk and Okolski (2008) based on the Labour Force Survey.

Table 6.7 Selectivity of acquisition and transfer of informal human capital by country of destination for Polish migrants

	Germany		The Netherlands		British Isles		Stayers	
	n	%	n	%	n	%	n	%
sex								
man	592	74.0	113	62.4	254	63.3	33654	50.1
woman	208	26.0	68	37.6	147	36.7	33520	49.9
FORMAL HUMAN CAPITAL								
job situation								
employed	542	67.8	104	57.5	272	67.8	48682	72.5
unemployed	98	12.3	36	19.9	56	14.0	5597	8.3
inactive	160	20.0	41	22.7	73	18.2	12895	19.2
year of birth								
1968–1982	290	56.5	67	48.6	163	52.8	27957	55.0
1983–1993	223	43.5	71	51.4	146	47.2	22871	45.0
self-employed (%)	15.9		9.4		10.7		14.4	
M net average income (PLN)	2473.88		2737.55		2723.06		1826.19	

	Germany		The Netherlands		British Isles		Stayers	
	n	%	*n*	%	*n*	%	*n*	%
M years in education	11.69		11.40		12.53		12.39	
INFORMAL HUMAN CAPITAL								
M job satisfaction	3.71		3.57		3.65		3.59	
M well-being	1.37		1.45		1.43		1.34	
M soft skills (IND)	3.35		3.39		3.62		3.40	
M soft skills (SOC)	3.80		3.80		3.95		3.86	

Source: cf. Grabowska and Jastrzębowska (forthcoming) based on BKL – Human Capital in Poland.

Migrants to the British Isles had the highest level of soft skills, both individual (M=3.62) and social (M=3.95), among the top destination countries for Polish migrants. This confirms earlier findings among migrants from Slovakia to the UK (Baláž and Williams, 2005) and Poles based Human Capital in Poland data set (Grabowska and Jastrzebowska, 2019). Several factors may be involved in this. First, the British labour market and British workplaces are open and agile and recognise the role of soft skills (cf. Heynes and Galasinska, 2016). Second, the English-speaking environment and the acquisition of communication and self-expression skills (cf. Baláž and Williams, 2005; Hagan et al., 2015; Janta et al., 2019; Baláž et al., 2019; Hagan and Wassink, 2020), and third, learning through observation, communication and action in teams (cf. Grabowska, 2018). Young post-accession migrants from Poland to the UK, many of whom were recent graduates, generally worked below their formal education level. This switch between completely different environments – going from university to working in a factory or the service sector – may have taught them flexibility and how to cope with boredom, and instilled a respect for manual labour and teamwork (cf. Grabowska, 2018). A fourth factor is the young age of Polish migrants to the UK and their mobile transitions to adulthood, also with a first job in life abroad and the achievement of financial independence (cf. Robertson, Harris and Baldassar, 2018). International migration helps them learn soft skills relating to combating adversity, autonomy and independence (cf. Janta et al., 2019).

The unique data source provided by the national representative survey on human capital, which allows for comparisons of movers and stayers, is available for Poland only. In this analysis (cf. Grabowska and Jastrzebowska, 2019; Grabowska and Jastrzebowska, forthcoming) we were able to list nearly all components of informal human capital from the model presented in Chapter 2, except maker skills.

Through factor analysis, Grabowska and Jastrzebowska (2019) were able to identify two components of informal human capital: mind skills (individual dimension) and soft skills (social dimension). Mind skills comprise the cognitive aspects of reasoning, knowledge and creativity, as well as critical thinking, information literacy, argumentation and innovation and the intrapersonal capacity to manage one's emotions and behaviours to achieve goals, including learning; it also relates to flexibility, initiative, appreciation for diversity and reflexivity. *Soft skills* concern the interpersonal and relational aspects of expressing ideas, interpreting and responding to messages from others, and also involve communication, collaboration, responsibility and conflict resolution. Polish migrants who returned to their origin country exhibited higher levels of soft skills and displayed greater life and job satisfaction.

Table 6.8 Stayers and returnees to Poland – mind and soft skills

	Stayers	Returnees
Informal Human Capital variables	Soft skills M=3.86 Mind skills M=3.40	Soft skills M=3.90 Mind skills M=3.45

Source: cf. Grabowska and Jastrzebowska (forthcoming) based on BKL – Human Capital in Poland.

Table 6.9 Stayers and returnees to Poland – life skills

	Stayers	Returnees
Informal Human Capital variables	Life satisfaction M=1.34 Job satisfaction M= 3.60	Life satisfaction M=1.41 Job satisfaction M=3.68

Source: cf. Grabowska and Jastrzebowska (forthcoming) based on BKL – Human Capital in Poland.

The Human Capital in Poland database is the only source of data that allows for identification of the life skills in our theoretical model, as presented in Chapter 2. What it does not reveal, however, is *how* international migration led to the development of these life skills.

We can only conclude that Polish returnees have higher life and job satisfaction than stayers.

Obstructing transfer

This section discusses the obstructing of MigCap transfer from both perspectives of a returning employee and a deportee; and from the perspective of employers employing returnees.

The Re-Turn research project (Lang and Nadler, 2014) studied the obstructing of MigCap transfer from the perspective of organizations in Central Europe.[5] Four assumptions were challenged in the study (Lang and Nadler, 2014: 82): (1) overall human capital hypothesis; (2) local rootedness hypothesis; (3) lower salaries hypothesis; (4) easy integration hypothesis.

With regard to the first hypothesis, they were able to confirm that return migration to Central Europe is associated with human capital transfer – both employers and employees notice its importance. As for the second, return migrants were shown to be a more promising workforce than other immigrants, particularly in rural regions. This is due to their socio-cultural proximity and understanding of local culture and conditions, especially linked to system transformation from communism to democracy in Central Europe. Concerning the lower salaries hypothesis, the companies interviewed reported that return migrants expect higher wages when they look for jobs in their home regions but most companies cannot afford to pay the expected wages. And finally, with regard to easy integration: local populations perceive return migrants as being "one of them", making it easier for them integrate into the community which was not relevant for studied companies. (cf. Lang and Nadler, 2014).

Other studies (van Mol, 2017) found that employers can also be insensitive to skills acquired abroad by migrants, which hampers the brain gain that could be derived from return migration (Dustmann, Fadlon and Weiss, 2011; Lulle, Janta, and Emilsson, 2019). Employers might be unsure about the value of foreign work experience (Hazans, 2008: 3).

The Re-Turn research project also studied the obstruction of MigCap transfer from the perspective of employees in Central Europe. An important migration literature is so-called "return of failure", which describes the return of migrants who are less successful in "taking an active part in the receiving societies or in adapting themselves to host societies" (Cassarino, 2004: 257–258). People are often unaware that they can learn a lot from a failure, and this is an indirect barrier to transfer.

> (…) most potential returnees expect a lot of difficulties, which implies a mismatch of experiences and expectations that needs to be addressed by return policies. However, less than 10 per cent of all emigrants know about return inititives (…). Some assume penalties whereas others expect rewards for experiences and skills acquired abroad. 39 per cent of returnees in the ReTurn sample report improved working conditions. On the other hand, about 27 per cent of the returnees have to deal with worse working conditions, 10 per cent suffer from labour market reintegration problems and are unemployed.
>
> (Lang and Nadler, 2014: 46)

Those who are willing and able to transfer MigCap are faced with challenges such as migration-related prejudice ("you think you know better because you worked abroad", "look who deigned to come back").

> Sometimes what we bring back from abroad cannot be implemented in the workplace in Poland. It is all stiff and traditional, impossible to be changed.
>
> (HARMONIA, research project, narrative of a returnee to Poland, female, 1980)

The perception of returning migrants as outsiders, newcomers, is also associated with the time of their absence – the longer they are away, the

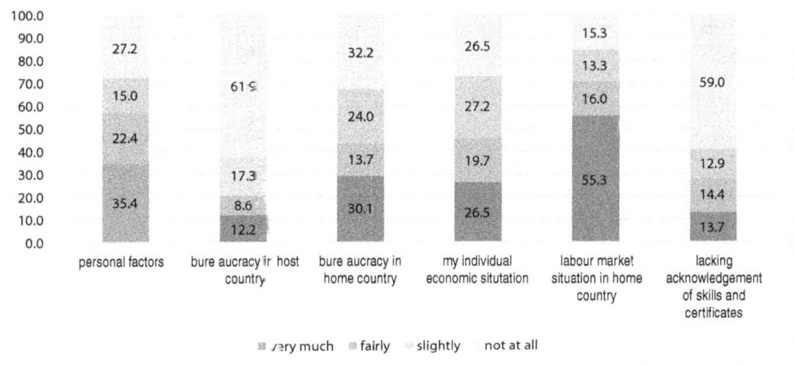

Figure 6.2 Barriers obstructing transfer of MigCap identified by employees in Central Europe
Source: cf. Re-Turn research project; Lang and Nadler (2014).

more they will be perceived as alien and socially inaccessible. Migrants may also find themselves relegated to peripheral positions in the organisation and experience difficulties being accepted by their co-workers. Another potential challenge is skill mismatch, i.e. migrants have acquired skills, including social ones, which may not yet be implemented in the workplace to which they have returned. Difficulties may also arrive from having to fit into well-established structures and patterns, as well as the power game in the organisation (Williams, 2007; Williams and Baláž, 2008b), which sometimes limits migrants in using the social skills they strengthened while working and living abroad. (cf. Grabowska, 2019).

In the DAINA CEEYouth research project the whole list of barriers to socio-cultural and economic reintegration after return was identified (see Table 6.10). We observed the similarity between Polish and Lithuanian returnees linked to barriers to reintegration after return (see Table 6.10). Over half of Polish returnees had difficulties getting used to the attitude of employers towards employees in Poland. Similarly, among Lithuanian returnees, over 47 percent of people experienced this challenge when re-entering the domestic labour market. It is also linked to the finding that every third Pole and Lithuanian had difficulty in finding a place in the labour market after returning. Other significant barriers observed in the DAINA CEEYouth research project include lack of cultural diversity at home and disappointment with customer service. Nearly every fourth Pole and Lithuanian also pointed out the lack of social contacts after return which means that their stays abroad

Table 6.10 Barriers to reintegration after return for Polish and Lithuanian returnees from the UK

Challenge	Polish Returnees		Lithuanian Returnees	
	n	*%*	*n*	*%*
Disappointment with customer service	286	55.4	121	58.7
Difficulty getting used to the attitude of employers towards employees in Poland/Lithuania	261	50.6	97	47.1
Lack of cultural diversity	220	42.6	71	34.5
Lack of cultural diversity	220	42.6	71	34.5
Difficulty finding a job	180	34.9	87	42.2
Difficulty in finding oneself after return	151	29.3	58	28.2
Difficulty using skills acquired abroad	150	29.1	62	30.1
Lack of social contacts/ acquaintances	118	22.9	49	23.8
Lack of social life one had in the UK	117	22.7	59	28.6
Difficulty obtaining social benefits	70	13.6	47	22.8
Difficulty obtaining a mortgage	47	9.1	35	17.0
Partner has difficulty adapting	42	8.1	24	11.7
Difficulty finding an apartment to rent	32	6.2	25	12.1
Children have difficulty adapting at school	32	6.2	15	7.3

The comparative Polish-Lithuanian survey with return migrants conducted in May–July 2020 within the DAINA CEEYouth; total PL n=516; LT n=206; only completed questionnaires. Source: Author's elaboration.

were long enough for many contacts to phase out and new professional contacts had not yet been made in their country of origin. The labour market situation in the home country was also one of the most significant barriers for reintegration after return identified in the Mexican research.

Comparing migrants who did not transfer soft skills with those who did in the data of the DIANA CEEYouth research project, we see that the former group contains more Lithuanian citizens and women, as well as a greater proportion of people who spent 10 or more years in the UK. Among MigCap holders, more people moved to larger cities.

Among Mexicans the most often reported challenges encountered after returning to Mexico relate to difficulty finding a job and low pay. One needs to notice however that more than every third never deported returning migrant to Mexico did not report any challenges (see Table 6.12).

Table 6.11 Comparison of migrants who transferred mind and soft skills and migrants who did not

Variable	Value	No transfer		Transfer	
		n	*%*	*n*	*%*
Country	Poland	205	69.5	311	72.8
	Lithuania	90	30.5	116	27.2
Gender	Women	222	76.3	294	69.8
	Men	69	23.7	127	30.2
Number of years in UK	1–5	101	34.2	174	40.7
	5–10	81	27.5	140	32.8
	10<	113	38.3	113	26.5
Residence	Fragmented: moved in and out of the country (min a year in the UK)	54	18.3	67	15.7
	Uninterrupted	241	81.7	360	84.3
Returned to the same place?	No, but I returned to a city / town of similar size	13	4.4	15	3.5
	No, I returned to a bigger city / town	39	13.2	101	23.7
	No, I returned to a smaller city / town	23	7.8	17	4.0
	Yes	220	74.6	294	68.9
Back to origin country	No, after leaving the UK and before moving to country of origin I lived in another country	23	7.8	37	8.7
	Yes	272	92.2	390	91.3

The comparative Polish-Lithuanian survey with return migrants conducted in May–July 2020 within the DAINA CEEYouth; total PL n=516; LT n=206; only completed questionnaires.
Source: Author's elaboration.

A very important group of Mexican returning migrants consists of deported migrants. Deportees to Mexico are stigmatised (Hagan, Wassink and Castro, 2019) after return. Empirical research suggests that "deportees are resilient and agile adaptable and they mobilise resources and skills upon return" (see also: Wassink and Hagan, 2018).

The research by Hagan and colleagues highlights the necessity of "study[ing] the post-deportation labour market experience as a dynamic

Table 6.12 Challenges encountered upon return by deported and non-deported return Mexican migrants (percent)

	Never deported n=74	Deported n=19
None	35	37
Difficulty finding work	25	21
Lack of education	5	16
Low pay	24	11
Employer preference for younger workers	5	16
Other	22[a]	21[b]

Note: Numbers do not add up to 100 because some respondents identified multiple factors.
[a] Other reasons reported by non-deportees: Discrimination because of tattoos, family difficulties, lack of savings, adjusting to life back in Mexico (multiple reports), the economy, lack of work experience in Mexico, lack of childcare, inability to transfer skills.
[b] Other reasons reported by deportees: social isolation after imprisonment in the United States, health, lack of skills and education, poverty (unable to afford goods/services), stigma associated with deportation.
Source: Hagan, Wassink and Castro (2019: 15).

social process in which human agency and skill mobilisation play a major part" (Hagan, Wassink and Castro, 2019: 2–3).

Return migrants to Mexico as deportees are often unemployed, having difficulty finding employers who will hire them and frequently turn to work in call centres, where they are often exploited but are at least able to use their English language skills and work alongside other social outcasts (Anderson, 2015; Golash-Boza, 2015). Hagan, Wassink and Castro (2019) identified the main barriers facilitating reintegration of deportees after return: level of preparedness for return, the way how employers receive them, employer preferences for an employee, high rates of poverty and limited opportunities for employment in the manufacturing and service sectors for returnees to mobilise and invest the resources they acquired abroad.

Meso and micro perspectives

The following sections of this chapter present our qualitative findings regarding the transfer of various components of MigCap. Informal human capital can only be transferred if it is recognised and valued by other people (cf. van der Heijden, 2002).

What content is transferred?

Mind and soft skills

The quantitative analyses presented above and our own analysis in Chapter 5 show that communication and English language skills are especially important components of MigCap transferred upon return. This applies to both Mexican and Central European migrants.

For returnees to Slovakia from the UK, English language skills were often interlinked with self-assessed improvements in self-esteem and social recognition (Williams and Baláž, 2005).

Box 6.1 Vignettes: returnees in Bratislava, Slovakia

Eva was a scientist working in the Institute of Hydrology in Bratislava. While she was doing a broadly similar job before and after her visit to the United Kingdom, she noted an important difference: "I am, however, more independent and my self-confidence increased. I think, people around me feel it."

Janka, an architect working in Dubnica had spent time in both the United States and the United Kingdom emphasized social recognition: "I think my friends and colleagues recognize that I became more experienced and professional. I believe this will soon be reflected in my income."

Lubos, a software expert from Bratislava gave a clear assessment of how the professional expertise he acquired was translated into an improved position, through a combination of self-confidence, improved communication skills and social recognition. "I think my social status improved after returning. I was promoted and became a senior software analyst. Now I can choose the work I like. Other people recognize me more than before. My pay increased as well. I speak good English and have no difficulty in communicating with other people. I also became more assertive."

Source: cf. Williams and Baláž (2005: 460)

The qualitative data about Polish migrants and returning migrants from the HARMONIA research project contained a number of cases in which individuals were able to transfer mind and soft skills. The majority of these had chosen self-employment after returning to Poland. The skill transfers they affected were confirmed by their bosses, employees, and friends.

The transfer of MigCap is strongly linked with social recognition which was repeatedly emphasized in their research by Williams and Baláž (2005, 2008b). Language and communication skills are most socially recognised, especially in post-communist societies, although opportunities to use them generally only exist in large and medium-sized companies (due to the greater probability of trade relations with foreign partners) than in small businesses, where the possibilities for skill transfer are limited due to infrequent international trade and the limited number of co-workers to interact with (cf. Grabowska, 2019).

For instance, a nurse in a private nursing home for the elderly and disabled people in local Poland transferred MigCap skills such as English and health-related communication skills; assigning the colours of uniforms for the patient and their family: doctor, nurse, caretaker; verbal and non-verbal respect for the patient: knocking on the room, respecting intimacy; holistic approach to the patient.

> I learned to knock on the patient's room. Oh, that was the difference. And I brought it to Poland. Even some were surprised.
> *In your work, do you sometimes introduce any things you saw there?* Well, I would like to introduce, I liked very much that these patients were offered bingo or a glass of sherry there in the evening. And here, however, only these pills, no entertainment and nothing nice. And yet the patients there … I would also like the hairdresser to come, beauticians to the feet (…) walk, do, see everything, this one. It doesn't. And it probably won't be long. But have you talked to anyone about this? I told the boss, he would love to, but how to do it. (…) And I always knock everywhere and wait a moment longer. And I think it's from England. Well, I always knock. Because this is the entrance to this patient's area. I think that's okay.
>
> (female returnee, born in 1978, a small town in Poland)

Another example relates to the pet shop owner and local activist in catholic organisations, donor of Single Mother House, active in children's school in Poland transferred to her social spaces – English and communicating; self-confidence and entrepreneurship attitudes and skills; the ability to speak out loud about difficult matters in the catholic church (IVF – in vitro fertilisation, domestic violence).

> (…) First of all, respect for the other, for the employee. The fact that I believe that if everything is done - this is what my boss in the UK

taught me - if everything is done, you can even read a book, but everything has to be done. And with me X has that she can ... She passed the driver's license now. But if it is, I do not require her, as I hear that the girls have to stand with a cloth and pretend that they are cleaning for eight hours, even though it is already polished, that they will make a hole soon. First of all, as much as I can, they earn really well, I think. X is happy, so ...

(return migrant, female, small town)

A teacher and owner of a paving company in local Poland transferred skills to his own company and the primary school where he taught. He transferred English and workplace communication; praising employees for good work; conciliatory resolution of conflicts between students at school (from experiences at the son's school in Northern Ireland).

First of all, I know what it looks like here. So it's easier to learn about English speaking countries, especially Great... and London. Maybe yes, let's start with London, because then the further, the difference. I believe that this experience gives me a lot more opportunities to communicate to students and tell what it really looks like and what to look for. It gave me a lot, because theoretically I am a philologist who speaks fluent English, but it turned out that when I came here, my English was too literary and I had to reject half of the things and learn such ... not necessarily correct English, but communicative. (...) It is also about the approach to the student.

(male returnee, small town in Poland)

A bartender and waitress transferred to her workplace – a pub and restaurant in local Poland – English and clear, task-oriented communication in a team (e.g. morning briefings at the workplace); time management; organising spaces and events; intercultural competences; responsibility:

(...) I am definitely trying to tell my boss about these morning staff briefings that it is cool. That maybe it would be nice ... Maybe not every day, because we are not used to it yet, but make such a short meeting once a week. Because the point is, keep it short, not tire us for a few hours and talk about what is wrong and what is not. Just short, say what we do well, what we don't do, and what else should be done to make it better.

(small town, return migrant, hospitality sector, born in 1990)

It is changing with migration, I have noticed a change in culture in restaurants – there is more customer care, more restaurateurs, owners go to the customer. There is no such thing as before that everyone had it: good, earnings, we have four letters.

(small town in Poland, female return migrant)

A handicraft female artist along with being an active parent in her children's school transferred communication skills to her environment, mostly to the school. These skills concerned various areas of life: in the family, in public institutions, including health care and in schools:

It is transferred. We come back and it transfers with us. This is a way, I don't know, of treating people, being open, more polite, smiling, making some kind of contact. Only we often have some such gloomy faces, passing each other. If you say "hello" or "what's up" and so on, they'll look at you quite strangely. Whether it's at the counter, at the store, at the station or anywhere. Not everywhere, it is changing slowly, absolutely. But in this respect, our culture, when it comes to young people who leave, older people as well – this is heaven and earth. Unfortunately, between them. And this is probably about … We have these adaptive abilities, if we go somewhere and want to survive, then we have to enter this culture, open up to it, so that it can become a little part of us and harmonize with it a bit, balance. That's the point too.

(small town in Poland, return migrant)

What I transfer after my return is the wish for a nice day to leave the cash register. And I wish you from Tesco a nice day, what I am doing and will be doing in Poland. And I think it's very good because it creates such a nice atmosphere.

(small town in Poland, female return migrant)

A local beautician in Poland who organised charity campaigns for nursing homes and orphanages transferred communication skills in servicing diverse clients in beauty salons; coping with emotional work; acting for the benefit of children and teenagers in need and understanding their needs.

A sports coach who returned from the UK to Poland transferred various communication skills. These included English and communication skills during sports training; encouraging people to participate in sports training with their family members – family integration.

In closing, we would like to summarise this section of this chapter with a quote from a returnee who talked about the transferral of soft skills after return.

> (…) their minds can be opened more. I would not like to claim some unknown merits, but it seems to me that this is the only role we can play - open up their heads. Yes? But are you doing it? You come to a small town in Poland and talk to your friends … - I'm trying. I think that my stories themselves seem to open them up. Yes? - Yes, I persuade each of them to come to me, visit me, not because I'm so lonely and in general, only on the basis of "man, you have to see this! Because I didn't believe it either".
>
> (a migrant in the UK, born in 1980)

Soft and maker skills

A mix of "maker" and soft skills and work habits increased the opportunities for returnees to do better on the labour market in their country of origin or to engage in entrepreneurial activities.

Some scholars have observed that human capital enrichment can cause circular and return migrants to become bearers of innovation and change, pioneers capable of creating entrepreneurial opportunities (Hagan and Wassink, 2016: 514). In other words, human capital can be used to create businesses in both innovative sectors and traditional ones. A number of studies have shown that the likelihood that migrants will set up a business after returning is positively correlated with the number of occupations during migration (Démurger and Xu, 2011) and the length of the period spent abroad (Mesnard and Ravallion, 2006; cf. Stanisia et al., 2019).

The non-financial human capital skills which migrants acquire abroad can influence their opportunities for entrepreneurship after return (Dustmann, 1999; Hernández-León, 2008). The following analyses aim to capture migrants' "total human capital," which is linked to formal schooling as well as, informal learning in social and vocational settings (Findlay et al., 1996; Hagan et al., 2015; Williams, 2007), which might impact their economic mobility after return (Campos and Lupián, 2015; de Haas, 2014).

Mexican migrants with little schooling often return home with enhanced technical and social skills that they developed in foreign work environments. Hagan, Wassink and Castro (2019) proved that Mexicans' human capital acquired in the United States, through reskilling and acquisition of new skills, predicted business formation upon return to Mexico. Then they showed that the learning of skills in the United States and subsequent transfer back to Mexico is enabled by skills learned in Mexico prior to migration.

Hagan, Wassink and Castro also showed that self-employed deportees benefited from skills learned in the US labour market. Other scholars found that Mexican migrants returning with savings and/or new skills acquired in the US labour market were more likely to succeed in the Mexican labour market, especially via entrepreneurship, than migrants who returned without skills and savings (Hagan and Wassink, 2016; Massey and Parrado, 1998; cf. Hagan, Wassink and Castro, 2019).

Factors that motivate engagement in self-employed activity after returning to Mexico include difficulty finding work, low education, and low-paid jobs.

Box 6.2 Vignettes: returnees in Leon, Mexico

Juan migrated to the United States in 2003 at the age of 23. In one of his U.S. jobs, he worked as an apprentice to a carpenter where he learned to use advanced machinery and install US-style kitchen cabinetry. After being deported, Juan opened his own carpentry business, installing U.S.-style cabinets using advanced machinery skills learned in the United States to improve the quality – and profitability – of his work.

Ana, who was deported only six months after migrating to the United States, did not have time to acquire new technical skills but she described gaining a powerful sense of self-confidence through the migration experience. Upon return to Leon, she opened a clothing boutique that carries US-style clothing. Five years later, she had expanded her business and hired three employees. Despite being forced home, both Juan and Ana benefitted from their US experiences, mobilising new found technical and social competencies into successful businesses that incorporated US building and clothing styles.

Source: Hagan, Wassink and Castro (2019: 14)

Box 6.3 Vignette: Hernando, Mexico

Hernando was born and raised in Heredia, a small agricultural community in central Mexico with an established history of emigration to the United States. He left school at the age of eight to help his father farm their land; 10 years later he landed an entry-level position at a nearby General Motors auto plant where he went through a six-month training program.

Despite the auto-making skills that Hernando learned on the production line, he grew tired of the repetitive nature of the work and, seeking adventure, decided to migrate to the United States, to Georgia where he had friends labouring in carpet manufacturing. However, after tiring of this similarly repetitive work, he found an apprentice position with a master carpenter. Through observation and informal on-the-job learning, Hernando became a skilled craftsman. After four years of working under the supervision of his mentor, Hernando had saved enough money to return home and launch his own woodworking business. Today he is the proud owner of a wood-working enterprise that provides US-style cabinetry and furniture to the growing return migrant population in his community. Like many other return migrants who launch entrepreneurial activities, Hernando mobilized new technical and social skills acquired in the U.S. labour market to train his employees and carve a new niche in the local Mexican economy.

Source: Hagan and Wassink (2015: 513–514)

Where and why is MigCap transferred?

The transfer of MigCap requires opportunity structures (Merton, 1996): social environments in which components of MigCap are noticed, recognised, valued and applied. The often low degree of social recognition of informal human capital contributes to their being bypassed by employers. The fact that migrants usually take low-status jobs while abroad contributes to this low social recognition of the soft skills they acquired in that time. The contributions of returning migrants to organisations are overlooked and not fully acknowledged.

The research findings of Hagan, Demonsant and Chávez (2014) among Mexican migrants suggest that job content and the industry in which learning occurs predict skill transfer.

> On- and off-the-job work experience in construction and automotive repair is easily transferable to the US and back to Mexico, where demand for these services is high. Other skills are place-specific and cannot be transferred (e.g., the techniques used in roofing and some

aspects of agriculture in the US are not applicable to work in Mexico), while others are easily transferable (e.g. metalworking, automotive repair, and English language skills), especially in large cities with a diverse industrial base and wherever demand for language capital is high.

(Hagan, Demonsant and Chávez, 2014: 95)

Research has proved that the acquisition of knowledge and work experience abroad can improve employability (Barcevičius, 2016; Williams, 2006), earnings (Dustmann, Fadlon, and Weiss, 2011; Martin and Radu, 2012) and occupational mobility (Hagan and Wassink, 2016) after return. However, at the same time, Martin and Radu (2012) also found higher probabilities of unemployment among Central Eastern Europeans.

When employers do appreciate MigCap, this can confer a competitive advantage. The tacit knowledge that migrants have gained in host regions can lead to competitive advantages for companies in their home country. Return migrants are considered drivers of product and process innovation and can provide new management models. Another important aspect is the maintenance of social relations with networks in the host country, which is required for return migrants to fulfil a bridging function between knowledge networks at home and abroad (Re-Turn research project; cf. Lang and Nadler, 2014).

MigCap acquired, strengthened and developed as a result of international migration can be effectively transferred in return locations, provided that the skills in questions can be shared through social contact with other people, and that the migrant's experience abroad, even if it involved work below their formal qualifications, is socially recognised or at least not dismissed.

For both Mexicans and Central Europeans, communication skills linked with English, but also with communicativeness, openness and opportunities to establish interpersonal and intercultural contacts are particularly valid benefits of migration.

What is important for both Mexicans and Central Europeans to transfer is the ability to take on challenges, self-confidence, work and cooperation in a socially diverse team. There does exist a paradox of sorts in this regard, however: on the one hand, employers seek to recruit employees with the mind and soft skills described above, and are therefore eager to hire migrants who have strengthened these skills while abroad; on the other, they do not always create or provide the circumstances and conditions required for the utilisation of these skills, which means that returning migrants are denied a social space in which these skills can be transferred.

Who transfers MigCap?

Agency and reflexivity are important and required features for non-material transfers of various components of MigCap. Active social actors develop these skills during their migration experience in order to strengthen their know-how, know-when, and know-what in a society.

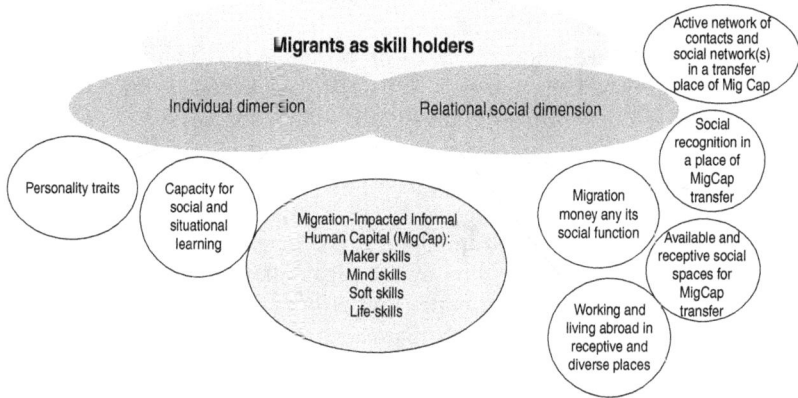

Figure 6.3 Migrants as holders of MigCap
Source: Author's elaboration; cf. Grabowska et al. (2017); White et al. (2018); Grabowska (2019).

The characteristics of migrants who engage in MigCap transfer could be classified into two dimensions: individual and relational (Figure 6.3). The individual dimension comprises personality traits associated with the capacity for learning socially while working and living abroad. The relational dimension includes having a network of active contacts at the point of transfer, social recognition and role in the space where the transfer occurs, the presence or availability of social spaces for transfer to occur in, work and life abroad in relational, socially diverse places, as well as migration money and its social value.

Summary

The acquisition of MigCap does not automatically provoke its transfer. Transfer requires a social space where MigCap – mind skills, soft skills, maker skills and life skills – is recognised, appreciated, valued and employed.

The MigCap – which both Mexican and Central European migrants declared to have transferred effectively in international social spaces – are communication skills. These are a combination of mind skills and soft skills: they consist of English language ability and interpersonal and collective communication in a team, organisation of work process and flow, the ability to follow and provide instructions, or dealing with emotional work in a customer service environment. In fact effective and clear universal communication know-how can be more effectively transferred than the mastered English language command itself as not many workplaces in migrants' home countries use English in their daily business, especially in local labour markets.

Mexicans reported more transfer of maker skills than Central Europeans, but clearly linked to soft skills. This is related to the sectors in which these groups primarily find work while abroad; while Mexican migrants tend to work in construction and agriculture, Central Europeans mostly find employment in the services and hospitality sectors (especially migrants to the UK).

We also learned that MigCap supports the transfer of entrepreneurship attitudes and skills for doing your own business after return. We found this not just among Mexican and Central European migrants (this development was most common among Polish return migrants), but also among Mexican deportees.

A more unfortunate conclusion is that with regard to life skills – the final component of informal human capital as described in Chapter 2, where we discussed theory (the other components being mind skills, soft skills and maker skills) – very little data is available about their acquisition and transfer among both Mexicans and Central Europeans. We were only able to learn that Polish returning migrants reported higher life and job satisfaction than stayers and greater care in maintaining a healthy work-life balance.

Finally, we were able to conclude that MigCap holders need available and receptive social environments to transfer their skills, as well as active social contacts and networks through which the transfer can be spilled over, and that the best skill transferors are international migrants who have a capacity for situational and social learning. It appears that specific personality traits also confer an advantage in this context, but further and more in-depth research would be required to draw any more detailed conclusions on this topic.

Notes

1 https://plato.stanford.edu/entries/capability-approach/ (accessed 20/12/2020).
2 "Returned migrants who reported owning their own business with one or more employees" (Hagan et al. 2015: 33).
3 POLPAN, the longest ongoing social science panel study in Central and Eastern Europe, focuses on describing social structure and its change in Poland. It was

begun in 1988 and is conducted in five year waves. The study is available at: http://polpan.org/en/.
4 The Matthew effect relates to an accumulated advantage according to the rule that "rich get richer and poor get poorer" (cf. Merton, 1968).
5 Countries under study in the Re-Turn research project: Czech Republic, Eastern Germany, Austria, Poland, Hungary, Slovenia, Slovenia, Slovakia,

References

Anderson, J. (2015). Labour Migration and International Trade. *Journal of Economics and Econometrics*, 58(3), 1–29.

Baláž, V. and Williams, A. M. (2004). 'Been there, done that': international student migration and human capital transfers from the UK to Slovakia. *Population, space and place*, 10(3), 217–237.

Baláž, V., Williams, A. M., Moravčíková, K., and Chrančoková, M. (2019). What competences, which migrants? Tacit and explicit knowledge acquired via migration. *Journal of Ethnic and Migration Studies*, 47(8), 1758–1774.

Barcevičius, E. (2016). "How successful are highly qualified return migrants in the Lithuanian labour market?". *International Migration* 54 (3), 35–47.

Biavaschi, C. and Elsner, B. (2013). Let's be selective about migrant self-selection. IZA Discussion Papers, No. 7865.

Borjas, G. J. (1985). Assimilation, Changes in Cohort Quality, and the Earnings of Immigrants. *Journal of Labor Economics*, 3, 463–489.

Borjas, G. J. (1987). Self-selection and the earnings of immigrants (No. w2248). National Bureau of Economic Research.

Campos, F. J. A. and Lupián, L. E. O. (2015). La migración y su influencia en el desarrollo del municipio de Parácuaro, Michoacán. *Cimexus*, 10(2), 35–48.

Cassarino, J. P. (2004). Theorising Return Migration: The Conceptual Approach to return Migrants Revisited. *International Journal on Multicultural Societies (IJMS)*, 6(2): 253–279.

Chiswick, B. (1999). Are immigrants favourably self-selected?. *American Economic Review*, 89(2), 181–185.

De Haas, H. (2014). Migration theory: Quo vadis? Working Paper 100, University of Oxford, https://ora.ox.ac.uk/objects/uuid:45aacf94-8f24-4294-9c74-cbc8453fcbfb.

Démurger, S. and Xu, H. (2011) Return migrants: The rise of new entrepreneurs in rural China. *World Development*, 39(10), 1847–1861.

Dustmann, C., Fadlon, I., and Weiss, Y. (2011). Return migration, human capital accumulation and the brain drain. *Journal of Development Economics*, 95(1), 58–67.

Dustmann, C. (1999). Temporary migration, human capital, and language fluency of migrants. *The Scandinavian Journal of Economics*, 101(2), 297–314.

Findlay, A. M., Li, F. L. N., Jowett, A. J., and Skeldon, R. (1996). Skilled international migration and the global city: a study of expatriates in Hong Kong. *Transactions of the Institute of British Geographers*, 21(1), 49–61.

Haynes, M. and Galasinska, A. (2016). Narrating migrant workplace experiences: Social remittances to Poland as knowledge of British workplace cultures. *Central and Eastern European Migration Review*, 5(2), 41–62.

Golash-Boza, T. M. (2015). *Deported: Immigrant policing, disposable labor and global capitalism* (Vol. 6). New York: NYU Press.

Grabowska I. and Jazwinska E. (2015). Migracje poakcesyjne Polaków i kapitał ludzki: transfer wiedzy, umiejętności, kompetencji. *Studia Migracyjne- Przegląd Polonijny*, 2(156), 53–80.

Grabowska, I. (2016). *Movers and Stayers: Migration, Mobility and Skills*. Frankfurt Am Main: Peter Lang.

Grabowska I., Garapich M.P., Jazwinska E., and Radziwinowicz A. (2017). *Migrants as Agents of Change. Social remittances in an enlarged European Union*. Basingstoke, London: Palgrave Macmillan.

Grabowska, I. (2018). Social skills, workplaces and social remittances: A case of post-accession migrants. *Work, Employment and Society*, 32(5), 868–886.

Grabowska, I. (2019). *Otwierając głowy*. Warszawa: Wydawnictwo Naukowe Scholar.

Grabowska, I. and Jastrzebowska, A. (2019). The impact of migration on human capacities of two generations of Poles: The interplay of the individual and the social in human capital approaches. *Journal of Ethnic and Migration Studies*, 47 (8), 1829–1847.

Grabowska, I. and Jastrzebowska, A. (forthcoming). *Migration-Impacted Informal Human Capital of Returnees*.

Hagan, J. C., Hernández-León, R., and Domonsant, J. C. (2015). *Skills of the "Unskilled". Work and Mobility among Mexican Migrants*. Oakland: University of California Press.

Hagan, J., Demonsant, J. L., and Chávez, S. (2014). Identifying and measuring the lifelong human capital of "Unskilled" migrants in the Mexico-US migratory circuit. *Journal on Migration and Human Security*, 2(2), 76–100.

Hagan, J. M. and Wassink, J. (2016). New skills, new jobs: Return migration, skill transfers, and business formation in Mexico. *Social Problems*, 63(4): 513–533, 10.1093/socpro/spw021

Hagan, J. M., Wassink, J. T., and Castro, B. (2019). A longitudinal analysis of resource mobilization among forced and voluntary return migrants in Mexico. *Journal of Ethnic and Migration Studies*, 45(1), 170–189.

Hagan, J. M. and Wassink, J.T. (2020). Return migration around the world: An integrated agenda for future research. *Annual Review of Sociology*, 46, 533–552.

Harzig, C. and Hoerder, D. (with Donna Gabaccia) (2009). *What is migration history?* Malden: Policy Press.

Hazans, M. (2008). Post-enlargement return migrants' earnings premium: Evidence from Latvia. Available at SSRN: https://ssrn.com/abstract=1269728 or doi:10.2139/ssrn.1269728.

Hernández-León, R. (2008). *Metropolitan migrants: the migration of urban Mexicans to the United States*. California: University of California Press.

Hodkinson, P. and Hodkinson, H. (2004). The significance of individuals' dispositions in workplace learning: a case study of two teachers. *Journal of Education and Work*, 17(2), 167–182.

Hochschild, A. (1979). Emotion work, feeling rules, and social structure. *American Journal of Sociology*, 85, 551–575.

Iglicka, K. (2009). *Powroty Polaków w okresie kryzysu gospodarczego. W pętli pułapki migracyjnej.* Warszawa: Scholar.

Janta, H. Jephcote, C., Williams, A., and Li, G. (2019). Returned migrants' acquisition of competencies: The contingencies of space and time. *Journal of Ethnic and Migration Studies*, 47(8), 1725–1739. doi:10.1080/1369183X.2019.1679408.

Kaczmarczyk, P. and Okólski, M. (2008). Demographic and labour-market impacts of migration on Poland. *Oxford Review of Economic Policy*, 24(3), 599–624.

Kanchier, C. (2000). *Dare to change your job – and your life.* Indianapolis: Questers.

Kolb, D. (2000). The Process of Experiential Learning. In R. Cross and A. Israelit (ed.). *Strategic Learning in Knowledge Economy.* Boston: Butterworth-Heinemann.

Lang, T. and Nadler, R. (2014). Return migration to Central and Eastern Europe: transnational migrants' perspectives and local businesses' needs. (Forum IfL, 23). Leipzig: Leibniz-Institut für Länderkunde e.V. (IfL). https:// nbn-resolving. org/urn:nbn:de:0168-ssoar-390656.

Lulle, A., Janta, H., and Emilsson, H. (2019). Introduction to the Special Issue: European youth migration: human capital outcomes, skills and competences. *Journal of Ethnic and Migration Studies*, 47(8), 1725–1739.

Lutz, W., Butz, W., and KC, S. (2014). *World Population and Global Human Capital in the 21st Century.* Oxford: Oxford University Press.

Martin, R. and Radu, D. (2012). Return Migration: The Experience of Eastern Europe 1. *International Migration*, 50(6), 109–128.

Massey, D. S. and Parrado, E.A. (1998). International migration and business formation in Mexico. *Social Science Quarterly*, 79 (1): 1–20.

Merton, R. K. (1968). The Matthew effect in science: The reward and communication systems of science are considered. *Science*, 159(3810), 56–63.

Merton, R. K. (1996). *On social structure and science.* Chicago: University of Chicago Press.

Mesnard, A. and Ravallion, M. (2006). The wealth effect on new business startups in a developing economy. *Economica*, 73(291), 367–392.

Naimark, H. and Pearce, S. (1985). Transferable skills: One Link Between Work and Family. *Journal of Career Development*, 12: 48–54.

Robertson, S., Harris, A., and Baldassar, L. (2018). Mobile transitions: A conceptual framework for researching a generation on the move. *Journal of Youth Studies*, 21(2), 203–217.

Staniscia, B., Deravignone, L., González-Martín, B., and Pumares, P. (2019). Youth mobility and the development of human capital: is there a Southern European model? *Journal of Ethnic and Migration Studies*, 47(8), 1866–1882.

Szymańska J., Ulasiński C., and Bieńkowska D. (2012). (eds.). *"Zaraz wracam.... albo i nie". Skala powrotów, motywacje i strategie życiowe reemigrantów z województwa śląskiego.* Kraków: CDS.

Tomescu-Dubrow, I. (2015). International Experience and labour market success: Analysing panel data from Poland. *Polish Sociological Review*, 3(191), 259–276.

Van Mol, C. (2017). Do employers value international study and internships? A comparative analysis of 31 countries. *Geoforum*, 78, 52–60.

Wassink, J. T. and Hagan, J. M. (2018). A dynamic model of self-employment and socioeconomic mobility among return migrants: The case of urban Mexico. *Social Forces*, 96 (3): 1069–1096.

White, A., Grabowska, I., Kaczmarczyk, P., and Slany, K. (2018). *The impact of migration on Poland: EU mobility and social change.* London: UCL Press.

Williams, A. M. and Baláž, V. (2005). What human capital, which migrants? Returned skilled migration to Slovakia from the UK. *International Migration Review*, 39(2), 439–468.

Williams, A. M. (2007a). International labour migration and tacit knowledge transactions: a multi-level perspective. *Global Networks*, 7(1), 29–50.

Williams, A. M. (2007b). Listen to me, learn with me: International migration and knowledge transfer. *British Journal of Industrial Relations*, 45(2), 361–382.

Williams, A. M. and Baláž, V. (2005). What Human Capital, Which Migrants? Returned Skilled Migration to Slovakia From the UK. *International Migration Review*, 39(2), 439–468.

Williams, A. M. and Baláž, V. (2008a). *International migration and knowledge.* Oxfordshire: Routledge.

Williams, A. M. and Baláž, V. (2008b). International return mobility, learning and knowledge transfer: A case study of Slovak doctors. *Social Science and Medicine*, 67(11), 1924–1933.

7 Conclusions and recommendations

Migration-impacted informal human capital (MigCap) is a distinctive form of human capital. This book does not seek to argue that it is of greater or lesser value than informal human capital unrelated to migration. In this monograph, we have argued that informal human capital is affected by international migration experience, and that this can result in new distinctive human resources. At the beginning of this book, we defined the concept of MigCap as follows:

> MigCap is an intangible multicomponent human resource comprising mind skills, soft skills, maker skills and life skills. It predominantly consists of tacit skills, though it also includes a number of explicit skills. MigCap is a non-validated, non-codified and non-certified human asset. It is dynamic; as such, it can be shaped throughout a course of migration. It can be acquired, developed, enhanced, mobilised, maximised, transferred, recognised, applied, utilised. It is migration-dependent in terms of type of migration, duration of migration, place of residence, job character and workplace environment. It may be affected by age/ birth cohort, gender, education and destination country. Not only means of MigCap are important resources and their conservation or maintenance but also ends – what people are going to do and can do with them.

In the subsequent chapters, we tested this conceptual assumption using both quantitative and qualitative data from different sides of the world: Mexico and Central Europe. This book, then, represents a detailed examination of the acquisition and transfer of skills acquired during international migration.

In order to explain the impact of international migration on informal human capital we used data from studies conducted on opposite sides of the world, among a variety of migrant groups: Mexicans and Central

DOI: 10.4324/9781003011545-7

Europeans, the latter consisting of Poles, Slovaks and Lithuanians. Unfortunately, these studies did not provide equal amounts of data for each of the research issues addressed, meaning that the analysis and discussion of certain aspects was more detailed for some countries than for others.

Care is needed in drawing conclusions about the impact of migration on informal human capital and its mechanisms, content and carriers.

We analytically reconstructed the mechanism of the flow of MigCap; in other words, what happens with MigCap in space and time. Using the available data, firstly, we analysed MigCap acquisition in the various countries of migration. Secondly, we analysed the transfer of MigCap in the country of origin after return.

The acquisition of informal human capital through international migration (MigCap acquisition) is the result of a learning process. When a person migrates with X resources, and comes back with X + Y resources, this means that their skills (a mix of mind, soft, maker and life skills) have increased by Y as a result of their international migration experience. This makes it possible to test a person in various new, unprecedented situations. People differ in their learning opportunities and capacities. As discussed in Chapter 2, Hobfoll's theory of the conservation of resources (Hobfoll, 1989, 2001) describes a so-called spiral of profits: the more resources a person initially has, the easier it is to increase their resources in subsequent stages of life. According to this theory, a person who has high initial social skills and who is highly reflexive will benefit more from migration experience. Another effect in play here is the Matthew effect: the higher a person's education level and position on the labour market, the more skills they obtain during migration. Such individuals are often goal-oriented innovator (Levitt, 2001).

The transfer of informal human capital as a result of international migration (MigCap Transfer) is the use of previously acquired knowledge and skills (i.e. acquired abroad) in practice. From the human perspective, transferring knowledge and skills and enriching one's life in its various domains, especially at work, requires at least two conditions to be met. Firstly, a person must be motivated to do so – if they have no desire present their informal skills to the world, said skills will remain invisible to others. Secondly, there must exist an opportunity structure (Merton, 1996): in other words, a social and organisational environment that enables individuals to freely share their skills with others.

One of our objectives in analysing the acquisition and transfer of MigCap was to determine exactly what is acquired and transferred; in other words, the content of MigCap. In our conceptual hypothesis, we distinguished between four categories of skills: mind skills, soft skills, maker skills and life skills. Our analysis showed that these do not stand alone and do not occur separately from each other. For example, we found that mind and soft skills usually go together, as do maker and soft skills. However, our data was too limited to draw meaningful conclusions about life skills in the areas of life and job satisfaction linked to well-being and work-life balance.

Through various quantitative and qualitative analyses, we established which categories of informal skills were particularly sensitive to international migration and therefore more likely to be acquired and transferred between destination and origin. These skills are presented in Table 7.1.

We also found out that in fact MigCap is very close to the human abilities catalogued for the 21st century.[1] It means that the experience of international migration can facilitate and stimulate a human with acquiring, developing and transferring the skills identified as necessary for living and working in the societies of the 21st century (Bell, 2010; Cedofop, 2012).

Table 7.1 The catalogue of international migration-sensitive informal skills

MIND SKILLS	SOFT SKILLS
- command of foreign language, mostly English - understanding orders, goals, aims - processing information - understanding know-how - rational and logical thinking and combining parts in a smart way - learning new things.	- teamwork - clear communication and communicativeness - customer service; emotion work - stress resilience - taking an initiative - leadership - entrepreneurship - creativity - being on time (punctuality).
MAKER SKILLS	**LIFE SKILLS**
- new construction techniques - machine operating - new solutions to old challenges and technologies - following smooth labour process; step-by-step - new work methods.	- making work stress-free - job crafting (matching job to own abilities) - work-life balance - mental health and safety conditions in a workplace - living conditions (e.g. simple life, eco life).

Source: Author's elaboration based on research findings.

Data-driven recommendations

In view of the comprehensiveness of our findings relating to the impact of international migration on informal human capital, we would like to humbly offer a number of recommendations for the benefit of policy-makers and decision makers in business organisations and public institutions. The results of the research findings described in this book are relevant from three perspectives: individual, organisational and global.

From an individual perspective, migration is often a journey into the unknown. It is not just about crossing territorial borders; above all, it is about crossing the borders within the human mind. Leaving their comfort zone helps migrants learn about the world and about themselves. When they return to their country of origin, the knowledge and skills they obtained travel back with them.

International migration experience not only affects the wealth of internal human resources, it is also significantly associated with higher work and life satisfaction. Our research shows that regardless of the country to which a person migrated, migrants – as our analysis of Polish migrants showed – have significantly higher life satisfaction than people who have never experienced international migration. Job satisfaction depends on the destination country.

Some people who have migrated and acquired MigCap return to the origin country, often to an organisation. Whether MigCap transfer subsequently occurs depends on two factors – the individual's motivation and the organisational climate, conditions and readiness for absorption and organisational development. Generally speaking, if a company is open to development, an employee with MigCap will be an excellent driver for it.

As part of this book, we would like to propose to various organisations the *Migration Skills Transfer Programme*. The aim of this programme would be to help organisations identify MigCap and opportunities and channels for its transfer in companies. Making use of this new capital may increase competitiveness, create an influx of new knowledge or help find alternative solutions to various organizational challenges at relatively low costs.

As we envision it, this programme would consist of three phases: (1) identification of the MigCap present in the organisation (firstly by identifying return migrants and their experiences); (2) recognition of the acquired migration skills (mind, soft, maker and life skills) of employees; and (3) transfer and application of MigCap in the organisation. The first phase is relatively simple and can be done in two ways – either during the recruitment and selection process, or through employee sessions at an Assessment and Development Centre (AC/DC). Subsequently, for the recognition of MigCap, we recommend individual interviews with potential or current employees who experienced international migration. In the third phase, MigCap transfer could be carried out through focus groups or other meetings and briefings with returning migrants or in individual mentoring or tutoring sessions.

Having a supportive organisational climate is a necessary condition to improve employee performance and encourage work attitudes behaviours in order to boost MigCap. Organisations should encourage and facilitate their employees in developing a positive work attitude and behaviour towards returnees with MigCap.

MigCap can be also used in national and international policy. It can help to emphasise that human capacities in the form of non-validated mind, soft, maker and life skills obtained through the course of international migration should be included as criteria for development of societies and their welfare. Policy makers may find it useful to include MigCap in priority policies addressing the development of human capital. The Migration Informal Human Capital Development Index (MHDI) is a summary measure of MigCap acquisition and MigCap transfer of human resources related to non-certified mind skills, soft skills, maker skills and life skills.

Table 7.2 Dimensions and Indicators of MHDI

Dimension	Cognitive	Personal	Manual	Well-being
Acquisition	Mind skills	Soft skills	Maker skills	Life skills
Transfer	Mind skills	Soft skill	Maker skills	Life skills
Indicators	Cognitive Ability Measures and Tests; job matching	Workplace engagement rates; productivity rates; staff turnover rates; impact on conflict; customer satisfaction; success with work process and flow (optimization); job matching	Assessment and practical skill testing; evidencing practical skills; job matching	Life satisfaction work satisfaction; job matching

Source: Author's elaboration.

Migration In formal Human Capital Development Index (MHDI) = MigCap acquisition + MigCap transfer

We would like to end with a final illustration of the usefulness of MigCap as a concept and tool: between 2019 and 2021 Izabela Grabowska collaborated with EY and the European Commission to organise and lead a research and social impact programme on the subject of return mobility for European Public Employment Services and EURES, in which she used the findings featured in this book.[2] We hope that in the near future we are able to facilitate both public and private institutions with Migration Skills Transfer Programme.

Notes

1 The ability to find a deeper meaning and significance of phenomena occurring in the economy and social reality; the ability to translate big amounts of data into coherent concepts and build data-based reasoning; the ability to compassion allows a human to understand the environment, influence reactions and enter into desired relationships with others; the ability to think and find solutions that go beyond the learned patterns; the ability to work and cooperate in various cultural paradigms; the ability to create and develop tasks, creative processes in such a way as to obtain the desired effect; the ability to cooperate effectively as a member of a virtual team; the ability to critically approach and develop content that uses new media and use these media for effective communication; the ability to give importance to information and increase its usefulness.
2 1st edition, *Return mobility,* 24–26 September 2019, Budapest. 2nd edition, *Return mobility,* 3–5 March 2020, Prague. Webinar, *Return mobility and pandemic,* 28 April 2020, EY for PES and EURES. 3rd edition, *Return mobility,* 28 September–1 October 2020, remote classroom programme for EURES and Public Employment Services. 4th edition, *Return mobility and pandemic,* 17–19 November 2020, remote classroom program for EURES and Public Employment Services. 5th edition, Return mobility and pandemic, 16–18 February 2021, remote classroom programme for EURES and Public Employment Services. 6th edition, Return mobility, 14–16 September 2021, remote classroom programme for EURES.

References

Bell, S. (2010). Project-Based Learning for the 21st Century: Skills for the Future. *The Clearing House: A Journal of Educational Strategies, Issues and Ideas,* 83(2), 39–43. doi:10.1080/00098650903505415.

Cedefop (European Centre for the Development of Vocational Training) (2012). Future Skills Supply and Demand in Europe: Forecast 2012. Luxembourg: Publications Office.

Hobfoll, S. E. (1989). Conservation of resources: A new attempt at conceptualizing stress. *American Psychologist,* 44, 513–524.

Hobfoll, S. E. (2001). The influence of culture, community, and the nested self in the stress process: Advancing conservation of resources theory. *Applied Psychology: An International Review*, 50, 337–370.

Levitt, P. (2001). *The transnational villagers*. Oakland: University of California Press.

Merton, R. K. (1996). *On social structure and science*. Chicago: University of Chicago Press.

Index

For Product Safety Concerns and Information please contact our EU
representative GPSR@taylorandfrancis.com
Taylor & Francis Verlag GmbH, Kaufingerstraße 24, 80331 München, Germany

www.ingramcontent.com/pod-product-compliance
Lightning Source LLC
Chambersburg PA
CBHW061323220326
41599CB00026B/5008